Sourcebook for the Performing Arts

Sourcebook
for the
Performing Arts

A Directory of Collections, Resources,
Scholars, and Critics in Theatre, Film,
and Television

Compiled by
**Anthony Slide, Patricia King Hanson, and Stephen
L. Hanson**

GREENWOOD PRESS
New York • Westport, Connecticut • London

Library of Congress Cataloging-in-Publication Data

Sourcebook for the performing arts.

Includes index.
1. Performing arts—United States—Directories.
2. Performing arts—United States—Bio-bibliography.
3. Performing arts—Information services—United States.
I. Slide, Anthony. II. Hanson, Patricia King.
III. Hanson, Stephen L.
PN2289.S65   1988   790.2'025'73   87–23630
ISBN 0–313–24872–9 (lib. bdg. : alk. paper)

British Library Cataloguing in Publication Data is available.

Library of Congress Catalog Card Number: 87–23630
ISBN: 0–313–24872–9

First published in 1988

Greenwood Press, Inc.
88 Post Road West, Westport, Connecticut 06881

Printed in the United States of America

The paper used in this book complies with the
Permanent Paper Standard issued by the National
Information Standards Organization (Z39.48–1984).

10   9   8   7   6   5   4   3   2   1

Contents

Introduction _____

Although there are many reference books on resources for the performing arts, we felt that there had been lacking heretofore a good, ready-reference source to provide the type of across-the-board information needed by most researchers. During the preparation of this volume, we realized just how many different books a researcher would have to consult to find names and addresses that would be helpful. It is our hope that this volume will appreciably quicken such research.

Sourcebook for the Performing Arts is concerned with the areas of theatre, film, radio, and television. Music and dance are included where there is an overlap into these areas, as in film scores.

The book is intended to provide documentation on collections and on individuals. The first section of the volume gives the names, addresses and telephone numbers of institutions with major holdings in the field, with brief descriptions of such holdings. The remainder of the volume is given over, primarily, to a who's who of leading academics, archivists, critics, historians, librarians, and scholars in the area of the performing arts. A listing such as the latter has never before been attempted, and, while there have been various volumes providing some information on resources in this area, it is the belief of the compilers that this is the first major attempt to compile such a listing for the entire United States.

An index provides ready access to all persons listed in the who's who section, and all institutions included in, and all collections mentioned, in the Institutions and Collections section.

Additionally, *Sourcebook for the Performing Arts* includes names and addresses of bookshops, journals and magazines, specialist publishers, major

United States motion picture and television studios and production companies, United States and international film commissions, television networks, and organizations. The last category includes guilds, unions, associations and institutions.

It is hoped that this volume will prove to be a valuable reference tool for scholars, students and librarians. Its list of collections should encourage research into lesser-known aspects of the dramatics arts, while the who's who should enable the reader to locate and become familiar with the work of major figures in the field.

The compilers would like to acknowledge the special help of Lisa Mosher in the preparation of this volume.

Sourcebook
for the
Performing Arts

Institutions and Collections _____

The following is a listing of colleges, universities, libraries, and other institutions in the United States with collections relating to the performing arts. Each entry includes the name, address, and telephone number of the institution, together with a description of its holdings, varying in length from one sentence to several paragraphs. Information is provided as to published descriptions of such holdings. Entries are arranged by state in strict alphabetical order according to the name of the institution, not the name of its library.

The following publications are recommended for additional information on collections dealing with theatre, film, radio, and television in the United States:

Allen, Nancy. *Film Study Collections: A Guide to Their Development and Use.* New York: Frederick Ungar Publishing Co., 1979.
Brady, Anna, Richard Wall, and Carolyn Newitt Weiner. *Union List of Film Periodicals: Holdings of Selected American Collections.* Westport, Conn.: Greenwood Press, 1984.
Gilder, Rosamond, and George Freedley. *Theatre Collections in Libraries and Museums.* New York: Theatre Arts, 1936.
Mehr, Linda. *Motion Pictures, Television and Radio: A Union Catalogue of Manuscript and Special Collections in the Western United States.* Boston: G. K. Hall, 1977.
Performing Arts Resources. New York: Theatre Library Association, 1974 to present.
Rachow, Louis A., ed. "Theatre & Performing Arts Collections," *Special Collections* 1, 1, (Fall 1981).
Rowan, Bonnie G. *Scholar's Guide to Washington, D.C. Film and Video Collections.* Washington, D.C.: Smithsonian Institution Press, 1980.

Wasserman, Steven R., and Jacqueline Wasserman O'Brien, eds. *The Lively Arts Information Directory*, 2d ed. Detroit: Gale Research, 1985.
Young, William C. *American Theatrical Arts: A Guide to Manuscripts and Special Collections in the United States and Canada*. Chicago: American Library Association, 1971.

Arizona _____

Arizona Historical Society
949 East Second Street
Tucson, AZ 85719
(602) 882–5774

The Society collects information relating to film making in Arizona and also has a number of oral histories with individuals, such as Yakima Canutt, William Clothier, Howard Hawks, Stuart Heisler, Ann Little, and John Wayne, associated with the industry here.

Arizona State University
Charles Trumbull Hayden Library
Tempe, AZ 85281
(602) 965–3415

The Library has the collection of writer and columnist Jimmy Starr, which includes various items relating to the motion picture industry from the twenties onwards.

California _____

Academy of Motion Picture Arts and Sciences
Margaret Herrick Library
8949 Wilshire Boulevard
Beverly Hills, CA 90211
(213) 278–4313

The Library has voluminous files on individual films, personalities, general subjects, and film festivals. Files contain clippings, photographs, press releases, programs, lobby cards, or other publicity materials. Among the more than four million still photographs in the Library are the collections of Thomas H. Ince, M–G–M, Paramount, Selig Company, and Mack Sennett. The largest studio-related collection is the Paramount Collection of stills, script materials and pressbooks.

Among the more than 100 special collections here are those of Richard Barthelmess (scrapbooks only), J. Stuart Blackton, Frank Borzage, Charles Brabin, Harold Bucquet, Maurice Costello, Duncan Cramer, Harry Crocker, George Cukor, J. Searle Dawley, Leonard Goldstein, Jean Hersholt, Hedda Hopper, John Huston, Joris Ivens, Jesse L. Lasky, Isobel Lennart, Robert Z. Leonard, Gertrude Olmsted, Louella Parsons, Sam Peckinpah, Lincoln Quarberg, William Selig, Mack Sennett, George Stevens, Technicolor Corporation, Hal Wallis, Perc Westmore, Jules White, and Adolph Zukor. Perhaps the rarest item in the Library is a letter from Sigmund Freud, in the Harry Crocker Collection, in which he analyses Charlie Chaplin's comic persona.

The Library also houses the Academy's archives, including documentation of all of the Academy Awards presentations, copies of various Academy publications, and publicity files on the history of the organization.

Ackerman Archives
2495 Glendower Avenue
Hollywood, CA 90027
(213) 666–6326

A major collection of more than 200,000 items relating to science fiction, fantasy and horror films gathered together by Forrest J. Ackerman, the archives include such esoteric material as props from *King Kong* and *Creature from the Black Lagoon*.

American Film Institute
Louis B. Mayer Library
2021 North Western Avenue
Los Angeles, CA 90027
(213) 856–7660

Although intended primarily to serve the needs of the students at the American File Institute's Center for Advanced Film Studies, the Louis B. Mayer Library is an important resource for books, periodicals, scripts and clippings relating to both film and television. It is one of the few libraries with a complete run, in hard cover, of *TV Guide*.

It is particularly rich in oral histories, with interviews on Pandro S. Berman, George Cukor, Allan Dwan, Howard Koch, Mitchell Leisen, Ray Rennahan, Donald Ogden Stewart, Crane Wilbur, and others. It also houses the interviews conducted for the Time-Life Audio History of American Movies, Richard Koszarski's interviews for his Erich von Stroheim project, transcripts of filmmaker seminars held at the Institute, and Donald Knox's oral history project on the making of *An American in Paris*. The Library houses a number of unpublished autobiographies, sponsored by the American Film Institute, and including those of Clive Brook, Oscar G. Estes and Rowland V. Lee.

Among the special collections here are the papers of Robert Aldrich, Claire DuBrey, Henry Hathaway, Harry Horner, Mitchell Leisen, Leo McCarey, Martin Scorsese, and George B. Seitz, as well as the Columbia Stills Collection from the thirties through the fifties, and the Jack Haley, Jr. Film/Video Study Center.

American Society of Cinematographers
1782 North Orange Drive
Hollywood, CA 90028
(213) 876–5080

The Society houses a small museum of artifacts on the history of cine-
matography and holds oral history tapes of a major group of pioneer ci-
nematographers: James Wong Howe, William Daniels, Arthur C. Miller,
Spencer Gordon Bennet, Karl Struss, Lewis Physioc, Philip Tannura, John
Arnold, Fred Balshofer, George Folsey, Roy Overbaugh, John Seitz, Harold
Rosson, George Mitchell, Charles G. Clarke, Arthur Edeson, Reggie Lyons,
Hal Mohr, James Van Trees, Charles Rosher, Joseph Ruttenberg, Henry
Sharp, John Baderacco, Joseph Walker, Gilbert Warrenton, Ray Rennahan,
Paul Vogel, and David Abel.

Anaheim Public Library
500 West Broadway
Anaheim, CA 92805
(714) 533–5221

As the home of Disneyland, the Anaheim Public Library, appropriately
enough, houses a Disney Collection.

Archives of the Performing Arts
War Memorial Opera House
San Francisco, CA 94102

A collection of papers, photographs, oral history tapes, clippings, arti-
facts, and programs relating to the history of the performing arts in the San
Francisco Bay area. For more information, see Gustafson, R. Eric. "The
San Francisco Archives for the Performing Arts." In *Performing Arts Re-
sources*, edited by Mary C. Henderson, vol. 6. New York: Theatre Library
Association, 1980.

Bison Archives
1600 Schuyler Road
Beverly Hills, CA 90210
(213) 276–9491

Bison Archives contain more than 60,000 film stills relating to the history
of motion picture studios.

Burbank Public Library
Warner Research Collection
110 North Glenoaks Boulevard
Burbank, CA 91503
(818) 847–9743

The former Warner Bros. Research Library is now operated as a commercial venture by the Burbank Public Library. It does contain some items relating to Warner Bros. films of the thirties and forties.

California State University
Urban Archives Project
South Library
18111 Nordhoff Street
Northridge, CA 91330
(213) 885–2487

Among the organizations that have deposited their papers with the Urban Archives Project are the Directors Guild of America and the Screen Cartoonists Guild.

California State University at Fullerton Library
Fullerton, CA 92634
(714) 870–3444

The Library houses the papers of screenwriter Fred Guiol.

California State University at Long Beach
Fine Arts Library
1250 Bellflower Boulevard
Long Beach, CA 90840
(213) 498–4023

The Library houses the scores from the M–G–M Music Library.

California State University at Los Angeles
John F. Kennedy Memorial Library
5151 State College Drive
Los Angeles, CA 90032
(213) 224–2212

The Library houses the papers, primarily scripts, of actor Anthony Quinn.

California State University at Northridge
Oviatt Library
18111 Nordhoff Street
Northridge, CA 91324
(818) 885–2832

The Library houses the film scores composed and/or arranged by Ray Martin.

Claremont Colleges Library
800 Dartmouth
Claremont, CA 91711
(714) 621–8150

The Library has the papers of lecture and theatre tour manager, Elbert A. Wickes, who worked with the Abbey Theatre players on their American tours in the thirties.

De Forest Memorial Archives
Perham Foundation
12345 El Monte Road
Los Altos Hills, CA 94022
(415) 948–8590

As its name suggests, the Archives hold the papers of the broadcast and sound film pioneer Dr. Lee De Forest, as well as the collections of Dr. Cledo Brunetti and other radio pioneers.

Fremont Library
39770 Paseo Padre Parkway
Fremont, CA 94538
(415) 791–4797

The Library possesses a collection of oral history tapes, newspaper clippings and books relating to film making by the Essanay Company and others in the community of Niles, California.

Henry E. Huntington Library and Museum
1151 Oxford Road
San Marino, CA 91108
(213) 681–6601

Several major collections here relate to the performing arts, notably the papers of Zoë Akins, Stuart Lake, John Fiske, and Sonya Levien. There is a collection of scripts from the "Gunsmoke" radio and television series, together with additional film and television scripts and various film stills and film-related photographs. The Jack London Collection contains items relating to films based on London's novels.

Historical Society of Long Beach
Rancho Los Alamitos
6400 Bixby Hill Road
Long Beach, CA 90815
(818) 422–6688

The Society has a scrapbook on the Balboa Amusement Producing Company, which was located in Long Beach.

The Hollywood Studio Museum
2100 North Highland Avenue
Hollywood, CA 90068
(213) 874–2276

The [Jesse L.] Lasky Barn, also known as the [Cecil B.] DeMille Barn, where in 1913 the latter filmed *The Squaw Man*, one of Hollywood's first features, has now been located opposite the Hollywood Bowl and is a museum providing a history of Hollywood, with particular reference to DeMille and Paramount.

Hoover Institution on War, Revolution and Peace
Stanford University
Stanford, CA 94305
(415) 497–2058

The Hoover Institution houses the records of the Motion Picture Council from 1927 to 1941. It also owns the Herman Axelbank Film Collection devoted to Russian history.

Institute of the American Musical
121 North Detroit Street
Los Angeles, CA 90036
(213) 934–1221

Although primarily concerned with the musical on stage and film, the Institute also has considerable holdings of books, photographs, clippings, and other material relating to all aspects of popular entertainment. It houses the archives of New York's Paramount Theatre from 1934 to 1951.

Los Angeles County Museum of Natural History
900 Exposition Boulevard
Los Angeles, CA 90007
(213) 746–0410

From the days when the Museum was simply the Los Angeles County Museum, it houses a number of collections relating to the history of Hollywood and the motion picture industry, among which are the papers of Edward H. Amet, Thomas Armat, the scrapbooks of Marion Davies, and the papers of William Farnum, Florence Lawrence, and Florence Turner.

Los Angeles Police Department
Office of Special Services
150 North Los Angeles Street
Los Angeles, CA 90012
(213) 485–3281

The Los Angeles Police Department houses a collection of materials relating to the television series, "Dragnet."

Los Angeles Public Library
630 West Fifth Street
Los Angeles, CA 90071
(213) 626–7461

The History Department here holds some photographs relating to motion picture theatres and the radio scripts from "Ralph Story's Los Angeles." Additional film-related photographs are housed in the Audio-Visual Department. The Literature and Philology Department has a number of film, radio and television scripts, as well as scrapbooks recording Los Angeles theatre history and an index to *The New York Dramatic Mirror*.

Loyola Marymount University Library
7101 West 80 Street
Los Angeles, CA 90045
(213) 642–2788

The Library houses the collection of writer Arthur O'Connell, plus a considerable collection of film and television scripts.

The Max Factor Museum
1666 Highland Avenue
Hollywood, CA 90028
(213) 856–6297

As its name implies, the Max Factor Museum is devoted to the use of make-up in the Hollywood film industry from 1904 onwards. The Museum is located in the old Max Factor Make-Up Salon.

McGeorge School of Law Library
3282 Fifth Avenue
Sacramento, CA 95817
(916) 452–6167

The Library houses a collection of scripts from the "Perry Mason" television series.

Michael Ochs Archives
P.O. Box 455
Venice, CA 90291
(213) 396–0202

A private archives devoted to the history of rock and roll from 1940 to the present, the collection includes photographs, films, posters, and books.

Music Center Operating Company Archives
135 North Grand Avenue
Los Angeles, CA 90012
(213) 972–7499

The nucleus of the Archives is the Raymond F. Barnes Collection of theatre memorabilia, which includes complete files of programs for the Los

Angeles Biltmore Theatre and the Los Angeles Philharmonic Auditorium, together with a card index to pre-1940 stage productions in the city. The Archives also collect documentation on the history of production at the Music Center and of the Los Angeles Philharmonic Orchestra, as well as materials on theatre in Los Angeles and New York. For more information, see "The Music Center Archives." *Performing Arts* (November 1977): 61–62.

Occidental College
Mary Norton Clapp Library
1600 Campus Road
Los Angeles, CA 90041
(213) 259–2852

The Library houses the papers of film publicist Barret C. Kiesling.

Pacific Film Archive
University Art Museum
2625 Durant Avenue
Berkeley, CA 94720
(415) 642–1412

Primarily noted for its nightly film screenings, the Pacific Film Archive also maintains a small, yet valuable, research library and a collection of more than 5,000 films available for viewing on the premises. The Archive is particularly rich in Japanese productions, and a catalog of the Daiei Motion Picture Company films in the Archive's Japanese collection was published in 1979.

Pacific Pioneer Broadcasters
Suite 609
6255 Sunset Boulevard
Los Angeles, CA 90028
(213) 461–2121

Pacific Pioneer Broadcasters has several collections relating to radio and television broadcasting, together with large collections of scripts, radio transcriptions, and oral histories. Perhaps the most important script collection here is that of Carlton E. Morse, creator of "One Man's Family."

Palm Springs Historical Society
221 S. Palm Canyon Drive
Palm Springs, CA 92262
(619) 323–8297

The Society houses extensive files relating to celebrities associated with the desert resort.

Palm Springs Public Library
300 S. Sunrise Way
Palm Springs, CA 92262
(619) 323–8298

The Library houses extensive files relating to celebrities associated with the desert resort.

Pasadena Public Library
285 East Walnut Street
Pasadena, CA 91101
(818) 405–4054

The archives of the Pasadena Playhouse from 1929–1970 are stored at the Pasadena Public Library and include photographs, box-office records, correspondence, programs, scrapbooks, and a run of the *Playhouse News*. Additionally included in the collection is the Billy Haas Collection of photographs of stars of the stage and screen from 1900 to 1930. For more information, see Nemchek, Lee R. "The Pasadena Playhouse Collection." In *Performing Arts Resources*, edited by Ginnine Cocuzza and Barbara Naomi Cohen-Stratyner, vol 10, 26–33. New York: Theatre Library Association, 1985.

Pomona Public Library
625 South Garey Avenue
Box 2271
Pomona, CA 91777
(714) 620–2033

Among the Library's collections of California memorabilia is the Padua Theatre (also known as The Mexican Players) Collection.

Producers Library Service
1051 North Cole Avenue
Hollywood, CA 90038
(213) 465–0572

Producers Library Service, founded in 1957, is one of the oldest and largest of independent stock footage libraries in the country, with more than 4.5 million feet of color film and 1 million feet of black-and-white film on file. The latter category includes more than 100 features films from the thirties and forties.

Riverside Municipal Museum
3720 Orange Street
Riverside, CA 92501
(714) 787–7273

The Museum houses the Collection of Lee Duncan, the man who discovered and trained dog star Rin-Tin-Tin.

San Diego Historical Society
Serra Museum
Presidio Park, P.O. Box 81825
San Diego, CA 92138
(619) 297–3258

The Society has a considerable amount of documentation relating to film making in San Diego.

San Diego Public Library
820 E Street
San Diego, CA 92101
(619) 236–5800

The Library holds a number of collections relating to local theatre production, along with an index to theatre reviews in the *San Diego Union* from 1851 onwards.

San Diego State University
Malcolm A. Love Library
300 Campanile Drive
San Diego, CA 92182–0511

The Library holds the papers, including films, tapes, scripts, and correspondence, of Desi Arnaz. The Library also has pre- and post-production
materials for the 1964 feature, *The Incredible Mr. Limpet.*

San Jose State University
John Steinbeck Research Center
250 South Fourth Street
San Jose, CA 95115
(408) 277–2745

The Center has a collection of scripts based on Steinbeck's works.

School of Theology at Claremont
Robert and Frances Flaherty Study Center
1325 College Avenue
Claremont, CA 91711
(714) 626–3521

The Center houses a collection of Robert Flaherty's films, as well as still
photographs, radio programs, and audio tapes.

Sherman Grinberg Film Libraries, Inc.
1040 N. McCadden Place
Hollywood, CA 90038
(213) 464–7491

Sherman Grinberg Film Libraries rightly bills itself as the "World's Largest News and Stock Library." It houses stock footage from the films of
Allied Artists, M–G–M and Twentieth Century–Fox, from the BBC "Wild-
stock" Library, from the television series "Nova" and "Odyssey," and
from the Paramount and Pathé News. A New York office is located at 630
Ninth Avenue, New York, NY 10036; (212) 765–5170.

Society of Wireless Pioneers, Inc.
P.O. Box 530
Santa Rosa, CA 95402
(707) 542–0898

The Society possesses papers, photographs, books, pamphlets, and periodicals relating to the history of communication and early radio.

Stanford University Libraries
Stanford, CA 94305
(415) 497–4054

The major collection here is the papers of Delmer Daves. There is also a
considerable quantity of scripts and photographs, and materials in the John
Steinbeck Collection relate, in part, to films based on the novelist's works.

Stanford University Museum of Art
Museum Way and Lomita Drive
Stanford, CA 94305
(415) 497–4177

The Museum has a major collection relating to the work of film pioneer
Eadweard Muybridge.

Thousand Oaks Library
American Library of Radio and Television
1401 East Janss Road
Thousand Oaks, CA 91362
(805) 497–6282

Founded in 1984, the collection covers all aspects of American broadcasting from 1920–1960 with special emphasis on radio. Included here are
complete runs of radio "fan" magazines, radio and television scripts, and
the papers of Carlton E. Morse, Fletcher Markle and Rudy Vallee.

Bruce Torrence Historical Collection
2336 Port Lerwick Place
Newport Beach, CA 92660
(714) 553–0800

A major collection of photographs relating to Hollywood as a community
and a film making center, the Bruce Torrence Historical Collection also

includes clippings, pamphlets, periodicals, and books on Hollywood history.

Twentieth Century–Fox Research Library
Box 900
Beverly Hills, CA 90213
(213) 277–2211

The Library serves as a research facility for use by studio employees and is not open to the public.

UCLA Film and Television Archive
1015 North Cahuenga Boulevard
Hollywood, CA 90038
(213) 462–4921

The largest film and television archives west of the Rockies, UCLA has an extraordinarily eclectic collection of films and television programs. (Despite the dropping of "Radio" from its title, the Archive also has considerable holdings of radio programs.) Among the film collections here, most of which consist of 35mm nitrate original prints only, are those of Warner Bros., Paramount, Republic, RKO, and Columbia. It also houses the Hearst Metrotone News footage.

Universal City Studios Research Library
100 Universal City Plaza
Universal City, CA 91608
(818) 777–1000

The Library serves as a research facility for use by studio employees and is not open to the public.

University of California at Berkeley
Bancroft Library
Berkeley, CA 94720
(415) 642–3781

Among the Library's collections are the papers of Rube Goldberg, Sidney Howard, and Harry Leon Wilson.

University of California at Davis
Shields Library
Davis, CA 95616
(916) 752–2110

The Library specializes in British and American theatre from the nineteenth century onwards and includes the papers of the San Francisco Mime Troupe, the Living Theatre, and critic Glenn Loney. Biographical files on film and theatre personalities are also maintained. For more information, see Sarlos, Robert K. "The Theatre Collection at Davis." In *American Society for Theatre Research Newsletter* 3, no. 1, (Fall 1974): 2–3, 9–10.

University of California at Irvine Library
Box 19557
Irvine, CA 92713
(714) 856–5212

A notable theatrical collection here consists of the papers of actress Helene Modjeska.

University of California at Los Angeles
Department of Special Collections
University Research Library
405 Hilgard Avenue
Los Angeles, CA 90024
(213) 825–4879

Major collections relating to the dramatic arts are housed in the Department of Special Collections, rather than the University's Theater Arts Library. Among the collections here are the papers of Hugo Ballin, Jack Benny, Eddie Cantor, Tony Curtis, Benjamin Glazer, Stuart Heisler, John Houseman, Ernie Kovacs, Stanley Kramer, Charles Laughton, Kenneth Macgowan, Ralph Nelson, Maria Ouspenskaya, James Poe, Paul Rotha, Sterling Silliphant, Albert E. Smith, Preston Sturges, and King Vidor. The George P. Johnson Collection is an important source of documentation on Blacks in the performing arts, and the papers of RKO Radio Pictures have recently been added to the Library. The UCLA Oral History program tapes of interviews with personalities involved in film, radio and television are also housed in the Department of Special Collections.

University of California at Los Angeles
Theater Arts Library
University Research Library
405 Hilgard Avenue
Los Angeles, CA 90024
(213) 825–4880

The Theater Arts Library houses a major collection of scripts, photographs and books. For more information, see Audree Malkin ed. *Motion Pictures: A Catalogue of Books, Periodicals, Screen-Plays, Television Scripts, and Production Stills.* Boston: G. K. Hall, 1976.

Special collections included in the Theater Arts Library relate to Tony Barrett, Gene Roddenberry, the Smothers Brothers, Andrew L. Stone, Haskell Wexler, and others, with each collection consisting primarily of script materials. The one major studio collection here is that of Twentieth Century–Fox, for more information on which, see Malkin, Audree. "Twentieth Century–Fox Corporate Archive at the UCLA Theater Arts Library." In *Performing Arts Resources*, edited by Ginnine Cocuzza and Barbara Naomi Cohen-Stratyner, vol. 10, 1–9. New York: Theatre Library Association, 1985. University of California at Los Angeles Music Library also includes collections of interest on General Music Corporation, Sunset Music Corporation, Harry Lubin, Henry Mancini, Alfred Newman, Alex North, Ernst Toch, and Edward Ward.

University of California at San Diego Library
La Jolla, CA 92037
(619) 452–2533

The Library has a collection of screenplays by Roy Harvey Pearce.

University of California at Santa Barbara Library
Santa Barbara, CA 93106
(805) 961–3420

The Library houses the papers of the city's best known resident, aside from Ronald Reagan, actress Dame Judith Anderson.

University of California at Santa Cruz Library
Santa Cruz, CA 95065
(408) 429–2801

The Library owns a collections of books, papers, and other material relating to Sir Henry Irving, gathered together by Robert McNulty. It also

maintains a collection of film stills and lobby cards, collected by Preston
Sawyer of the Santa Cruz *Sentinel*.

University of Redlands
Armacost Library
1200 East Colton Avenue
Redlands, CA 92373
(714) 793–2121

The Library houses a collection of film and television scripts by Charles
A. Wallace.

University of Santa Clara
Orradre Library
Santa Clara, CA 95053
(408) 984–4415

The Library has a collection of scripts from the "Daniel Boone" television
series and a collection of music scores for films by Lionel Newman.

University of Southern California
Department of Special Collections
Doheny Library
University Park
Los Angeles, CA 90007
(213) 743–6362

Among the collections here are the papers of Steve Allen, Edward Anhalt,
Jim Backus, Fay Bainter, Charles Bickford, John Brahm, George Burns
and Gracie Allen, Chuck Connors, Dame Gladys Cooper, Joseph Cotten,
Don DeFore, William C. de Mille, Andy Devine, Billy De Wolfe, William
Dieterle, Philip Dunne, Dan Duryea, Nelson Eddy, Roger Edens, William
Farnum, Richard Fleischer, Theodore J. Flicker, Arthur Freed, Clark Gable,
Tay Garnett, Freeman Gosden and Charles Correll (Amos 'n' Andy), Robert
Hamner, Charles Higham, Hal Humphrey, Ernest Lehman, Sol Lesser,
Boris Leven, Albert Lewin, Jerry Lewis, Jack Lord, Abby Mann, Virginia
Mayo, Jack Oakie, Joseph Pasternak, Ronald Reagan, Cesar Romero, Sid-
ney Sheldon, Robert Sisk, Anthony Slide, Edward Small, John Stahl, An-
drew L. Stone, Dimitri Tiomkin, King Vidor, Lawrence Weingarten, Claire
Windsor, Robert Wise, and Fay Wray.
    There are two major studio collections here: 20,000 scripts in the

M–G–M Screenplay Collection, covering the years 1918–1958; and the massive Warner Bros. Collection. For more information on the latter, see Yeck, Joanne. "Verbal Messages Cause Misunderstanding and Delays (Please Put Them in Writing): The Warner Bros. Collection." In *Performing Arts Resources*, edited by Ginnine Cocuzza and Barbara Naomi Cohen-Stratyner, vol. 10, 10–15. New York: Theatre Library Association, 1985.

The Library also houses clippings files, books on the dramatic arts, and a major periodical collection, which is particularly rich in foreign language publications. For more information, see Wheaton, Christopher D. and Richard B. Jewell, comps. *Primary Cinema Resources: An Index to Screenplays, Interviews and Special Collections at the University of Southern California*, Boston: G. K. Hall, 1975.

Variety Arts Center
940 South Figueroa Street
Los Angeles, CA 90015
(213) 623–9100

The Variety Arts Center houses a good collection of books on the performing arts, along with Eddie Cantor's gag files and correspondence, the Earl Carroll Collection, one of Buster Keaton's scrapbooks, and almost complete runs in hard copy of *TV Guide* and *Variety* (from the thirties through the fifties).

Walt Disney Archives
500 South Buena Vista Street
Burbank, CA 91521
(818) 840–1000

Housed in the Roy O. Disney Building on the studio lot, the Disney Archives were established in 1970 and include all of Walt Disney's office correspondence from 1930 to 1960, Walt Disney's personal memorabilia, Disney publications, publicity materials from 1924, 500,000 photographs, production files, oral history, original artwork, and documentation on the Disney theme parks. There are a number of special indexes and files to help researchers.

For more information, see Smith, David R. "Archives of the Mouse Factory." In *Performing Arts Resources*, edited by Mary C. Henderson, vol. 6, 94–96. New York: Theatre Library Association, 1980.

William S. Hart Ranch
24151 Newhall Avenue
Newhall, CA 91355
(805) 259–0855

Although primarily a tourist attraction, the Ranch does house scrapbooks, films, and other items relating to the career of William S. Hart.

Colorado _____

Denver Public Library
1357 Broadway
Denver, CO 80203
(303) 571–2000

The Library is particularly rich in materials relating to entertainment as part of Western history, with items on Buffalo Bill Cody, vaudeville, Chautauqua, and other subjects.

State Historical Society of Colorado
200 14th Avenue
Denver, CO 80203
(303) 892–2305

The Society has materials relating to film, theatre, radio, and television in Colorado.

University of Colorado
Rocky Mountain Film Center
Hunter 102
Boulder, CO 80309
(303) 492–7903

A media center concerned with developing the resources and information necessary for film study in the Rocky Mountain states, the Center does maintain a small library of books and periodicals, as well as a collection of 16mm films.

Connecticut _____

Bridgeport Public Library
Fine Arts Department
925 Broad Street
Bridgeport, CT 06614
(203) 576–7412

The Library houses files of photographs and clippings—more than 500,000 items—relating to theatre and the motion picture.

Eugene O'Neill Memorial Theater Center, Inc.
325 Pequot Avenue
New London, CT 06320
(203) 443–0051

As its name suggests, the Center is primarily concerned with the collection of documentation on the career of playwright Eugene O'Neill. Among additional collections here are those of Johnson Briscoe, the National Theater of the Deaf scripts, Virginia Dean, and the Harold Friedlander Playbill Collection.

Wesleyan University
Cinema Archives
Middletown, CT 06457
(203) 347–9411

Founded in 1985, the Wesleyan Cinema Archives have quickly built up an impressive array of collections, including the papers of Frank Capra, Elia Kazan, Ingrid Bergman, Kay Francis, Raoul Walsh, William Hornbeck, and Robert Saudek. The last includes the entire kinescope collection of the "Omnibus" television series. Additionally, the Archives hold film-related books, posters and photographs.

Yale University
School of Drama Library
222 York Street
Yale Station, Box 1903A
New Haven, CT 06520
(203) 436–2213

The Library collects photographs, books, plays, costume and set designs, scrapbooks, and periodicals.

Yale University
Sterling Memorial Library
New Haven, CT 06520
(203) 436–0907

Among the collections here are the papers of critic Dwight Macdonald and the J. R. Crawford Theater Collection. There are approximately 40,000 theatre programs from the seventeenth century onwards, and additional drama-related material may be found in the Yale Collection of American Literature. Yale University is also the repository for the John Griggs film collection, a magnificent group of 16mm features and short subjects, many of which are either rare or unique.

District of Columbia _____

Broadcast Pioneers Library
1771 N Street N.W.
Washington, DC 20036
(202) 223–0088

The Library includes books, pamphlets, periodicals, photographs, and more than 500 oral histories.

Folger Shakespeare Library
201 East Capitol Street
Washington, DC 20003
(202) 544–4600

The Library contains the world's largest collection of original editions and reprints of Shakespeare's works, as well as works by Restoration playwrights. Other holdings include the Smock Alley Theatre collection of promptbooks, the promptbooks of Augustin Daly, George Beck, Edward Sothern, and John Moore, the records of the Drury Lane Theatre (London) from 1766 to 1880, the notebooks of James Winston, the correspondence files of Augustin Daly and William Winter, and 300 of David Garrick's letters. Theatrical scrapbooks cover the years 1750 to 1920. Additionally, the Library has a collection of some 100 films based on Shakespeare's works. The holdings of the Library are listed in *Catalog of Printed Books of the Folger Shakespeare Library*, Boston: G. K. Hall, 1970, and *Catalog of Manuscripts of the Folger Shakespeare Library*, Boston: G. K. Hall, 1971. For more information, see Krivasky, Nati H. and Laetitia Yeandle. "Theatrical Holdings of the Folger Shakespeare Library." In *Performing Arts Resources*, edited by Ted Perry, vol. 1, 48–55. New York: Drama Book Specialists and the Theatre Library Association, 1975.

Georgetown University
Lauinger Library
37th and O Streets, N.W.
Washington, DC 20057
(202) 625–3230

The Eugene McCarthy Historical Project Archive contains a considerable amount of film, videotape, and photographs. More than 50,000 film stills are included in the Quigley Publications Archives, and the Wilfred Parsons, S. J. Collection contains items relating to the National Legion of Decency.

George Washington University Library
Television News Study Center
2130 H. Street N.W.
Washington, DC 20052
(202) 676–6378

As its name suggests, the Center compiles documentation dealing with television news.

Howard University
Channing Pollock Theatre Collection
Washington, DC 20059
(202) 636–7259

Founded in 1950 and named after the late playwright and critic, the Channing Pollock Theatre Collection includes photographs, playbills, programs, autographed letters, and manuscripts. Aside from the library and papers of Channing Pollock, the collection also includes the scrapbooks of Olga Nethersole, the Percy G. Williams Collection, the Alfred H. Woods Collection of theatre contracts, the Roland Reed Collection of playbills, and the Albert Berkowitz Collection of photographs from London's Old Vic Company.

John F. Kennedy Center for the Performing Arts
The Performing Arts Library
Washington, DC 20566
(202) 287–6245

The Performing Arts Library provides a general collection of books and periodicals on theatre, music, dance, and broadcasting and also houses a collection of clippings and programs relating to productions at the Center.

Library of Congress
Washington, DC 20540
(202) 287–5000

As the nation's copyright depository, the Library of Congress has been collecting films since 1894, and these have become part of the National Film Collection, housed in the Motion Picture, Broadcasting, and Recorded Sound Division. The Division's holdings include radio and television programs, together with the country's largest collection of films. Among the major holdings here are the productions of Columbia Pictures, Warner Bros., RKO Radio Pictures, Universal Pictures, and the American Film Institute Collection. The last is detailed in *Catalog of Holdings; the American Film Institute Collection and the United Artists Collection at the Library of Congress*, Washington, DC.: The American Film Institute, 1978. The papers and films of pioneer distributor George Kleine, held by the Library, are documented in *The George Kleine Collection of Early Motion Pictures in the Library of Congress: A Catalog*, compiled by Rita Horwitz and Harriet Harrison, and published by the Library of Congress in 1980. The Motion Picture, Broadcasting, and Recorded Sound Division also maintains a reference library in its own reading room, including runs of *The Moving Picture World* and *Motion Picture News*.

The Library's Music Division houses the papers of Geraldine Farrar, and also, thanks to the Copyright Act, has an extraordinary collection of film and theatre scores. Among other collections in this division are the papers of George Antheil, George and Ira Gershwin, Oscar Hammerstein II, Victor Herbert, Richard Rodgers, and Sigmund Romberg.

The Manuscript Division houses the papers of Lillian Gish, Ruth Gordon, Garson Kanin, Arnold Moss, Groucho Marx, Miriam Cooper, Vincent Price, Rod Serling, May Robson, Clarence E. Mulford (the creator of Hopalong Cassidy), and Hume Cronyn and Jessica Tandy. A recent addition is the archives and records of Washington's Ford Theatre. A general overview of collections at the Library of Congress is provided in *Special Collections in the Library of Congress*, published by the U.S. Government Printing Office in 1981.

National Geographic Society
Stock Film Library
1145 17 Street NW
Washington, DC 20036
(202) 857–7660

The Library makes available for sale, at commercial rates, footage shot for the various National Geographic television programs.

U.S. National Archives and Records Service
Pennsylvania Avenue
Washington, DC 20408
(202) 523–3010

The National Archives and Records Service is the major source for government-sponsored film footage, together with other documentary and news footage. In the latter category, major collections consist of *Paramount News* from 1941 to 1957, *Movietone News* from 1957 to 1963, *Universal News* from 1946 to 1967, *The March of Time* from 1939 to 1951, the Ford Film Collection from 1914 to 1956, CBS news broadcasts from 1974, NBC news broadcasts from 1976, ABC news broadcasts from 1977, and documentaries from the Second World War.

Florida _____

University of Florida Libraries
Belknap Collection for the Performing Arts
512 Library West
Gainesville, FL 32611
(904) 392–0322

Founded in 1953 as the Dance and Music Archives, the basis for this collection is material gathered by Sara Yancey Belknap. It includes clippings, posters, playbills, programs, flyers, books, prints, and photographs. Also part of the Collection is the Ringling Museum Theatre Collection. For more information, see Correll, Laraine. "The Belknap Collection of Performing Arts: University of Florida Libraries." In *Performing Arts Resources*, edited by Ted Perry, vol. 1, 56–65. New York: Drama Book Specialists and the Theatre Library Association, 1975.

University of South Florida Library
Tampa, FL 33620
(813) 974–2732

The Library houses a major manuscript collection on playwright Dion Boucicault.

Georgia _____

Emory University
Robert W. Woodruff Library
Atlanta, GA 30322
(404) 329–6887

The Library's collection of the papers of Lady Gregory includes unique documentation on Dublin's Abbey Theatre.

The *Gone with the Wind* Museum
152 Nassau Street, N.W.
Atlanta, GA 30303
(404) 522–1526

Nothing more or less than its name implies, the Museum claims to possess the largest collection in the world of *Gone with the Wind* memorabilia.

University of Georgia
Special Collections Library
Athens, GA 30602
(404) 542–2972

The Library has a considerable collection of books, pamphlets, periodicals, film stills, posters, and 16mm films. It houses the collections of actor

Charles Coburn and theatre critic and writer Ward Morehouse, together with an extensive collection of materials relating to the Paris Music Hall. It has built up a collection of scripts, and other material relating to films set in Georgia (including *Gone with the Wind*). In the area of radio and television, it maintains the George Foster Peabody Radio-TV Awards Collection and owns the Arbitron television and radio program ratings from 1949 to the present.

Idaho _____

Idaho State University
Speech and Drama Department
Pocatello, ID 83209
(208) 236–3695

The University houses the papers of noted costume designer Edward Stevenson.

Illinois _____

Chicago Historical Society
Clark Street at North Avenue
Chicago, IL 60614
(312) 642–4600

The Society has a collection of more than 12,000 theatre programs.

Chicago Public Library Cultural Center
78 East Washington Street
Chicago, IL 60602
(312) 269–2926

Although the Library is disappointing in that it does not have documentation on Chicago's early film companies, it does house the Goodman Theater Archives, together with forty scrapbooks on Chicago theatre history.

Newberry Library
60 West Walton Street
Chicago, IL 60610
(312) 943–9090

The Library's holdings include the papers of Sherwood Anderson and Ben Hecht, the Midwest Dance Archive, and considerable material on the Little Theatre Movement.

Northwestern University Library
Evanston, IL 60201
(312) 491–3354

The Library is the proud possessor of the complete archives of the Gate Theatre, Dublin. For more information, see Howe, Ellen V. "The Dublin Gate Theatre at Northwestern University Library." In *Performing Arts Resources*, edited by Ginnine Cocuzza and Barbara Naomi Cohen-Stratyner, vol. 10, 34–39. New York: Theatre Library Association, 1985.

Southern Illinois University
Delyte W. Morris Library
Carbondale, IL 62901
(618) 453–2522

Among the University's holdings are the papers of Katherine Dunham, Mordecai Gorelik, John Howard Lawson, and Erwin Piscator.

Theatre Historical Society of America
2215 W. North Avenue
Chicago, IL 60647
(312) 252–7200

Aside from publishing its excellent quarterly, *Marquee*, the Theatre Historical Society of America maintains a library of photographs, programs, and periodicals relating to the history of the motion picture theatre.

University of Illinois Library
1408 West Gregory Drive
Urbana, IL 61801
(217) 333–3777

The Library houses a fine collection of books, film stills, periodicals, and scripts. A listing of the last was published as Allen, Nancy, and Robert Carringer. *Annotated Catalog of Unpublished Film and Television Scripts in the University of Illinois Library at Urbana-Champaign.* Urbana: University of Illinois, 1986. Among the major collections here are the papers of Samson Raphaelson, Ben Hecht, and Fritz Leiber. The Library also has more than 3,000 theatre programs and photographs, from 1871 to 1930, in the Alyene Westfall Prehn Collection, the WGN Music Collection, and a collection of eighteenth- and nineteenth-century theatre prints. The papers of Joseph T. Tykociner, one of the early experimenters of sound on film, are also housed on campus.

Indiana _____

Indiana University
Black Culture Center
109 North Jordan Avenue
Bloomington, IN 47405
(812) 335–9271

Materials here relate, in part, to Blacks in film, music and drama.

Indiana University
Lilly Library
Bloomington, IN 47405
(812) 335–2452

The Lilly Library has become a major resource for study of the Golden Age of American cinema with the acquisition of the papers of two of this country's most important directors, John Ford and Orson Welles. Additionally, the Library has documentation relating to the BBC's Third Program (which brought culture to the radio), the papers of television writer John McGreevey, approximately 2,300 photographs from Sergei Eisenstein's *Thunder over Mexico*, and a small number of memoranda and notes from Darryl F. Zanuck. The Will Hays collection here is available on microfilm from University Publications of America.

Indiana University
Oral History Research Center
512 North Fess
Bloomington, IN 47401
(812) 335–2856

The Center possesses a transcribed oral history with actor Melvyn Douglas, together with various oral histories detailing the history of twentieth-century theatre in the United States.

Iowa _____

Iowa State University Library
American Archives of the Factual Film
Ames, IA 50011
(515) 294–6672

The Archives consist of a film collection, books, periodicals, scripts, catalogs, promotional materials, and correspondence relating to the factual film.

University of Iowa Library
Iowa City, IA 52242
(319) 353–4450

Among the Library's holdings are the papers of Robert Blees, David Swift, Albert J. Cohen, and Albert Zugsmith, all of which consist primarily of screenplays. Additionally, the Library has voluminous materials relating to the Victor Animatograph Company, the records of New York's Roxy Theatre, and approximately 2,000 scripts from Twentieth Century–Fox. The Library is an essential resource for the study of vaudeville history thanks to its acquisition of the B. F. Keith Collection, which includes clippings, books, files, and posters.

Kansas _____

Independence Community Junior College
College Avenue and Brookside Drive
Independence, KS 67301
(316) 331–4100

William Inge, who was born in Independence, donated a number of his original manuscripts to this College, which has also acquired a certain amount of Inge memorabilia.

Kentucky

University of Louisville
Department of Rare Books and Special Collections
Belknap Campus
Louisville, KY 40292
(502) 588–6762

Theatrical collections here include the programs of Louisville's Macauley Theatre from 1880 to 1912 and the Boyd Martin Collection of promptbooks, photographs, and scrapbooks. Additionally, the University is the repository of more than 20,000 items in the collection of British film critic and writer Roger Manvell.

Maine

Boothbay Theatre Museum
Corey Lane
Boothbay, ME 04537
(207) 633–4536

Assembled by Franklyn Lenthall and James Wilmot, the Boothbay Theatre Museum houses theatrical artifacts from the eighteenth century onwards, as well as research files of newspaper clippings, correspondence, autographs, theatrical journals, playbills, and prints. Among the items on display are Edwin Booth's *Hamlet* costume and the cape worn by Margaret Rutherford as "Miss Marple." For more information, see Lenthall, Franklyn. "The Theatre Museum, Boothbay, Maine." In *Theatre & Performing Arts Collections.* 1, 1, (Fall 1981): 99–112. Special Collections Series, Louis A. Rachow, ed. New York: The Haworth Press.

Maryland _____

Maryland Historical Society
201 West Monument Street
Baltimore, MD 21201
(301) 685–3750

Housed here are the papers of Eubie Blake.

Massachusetts _____

Amherst College
Robert Frost Library
Amherst, MA 01002
(413) 542–2212

Among the theatre-related special collections held by Amherst College are those of Augustin Daly, Clyde Fitch, Eugene O'Neill, and George A. Plimpton.

Boston University
Mugar Memorial Library
771 Commonwealth Avenue
Boston, MA 02215
(617) 353–3696

Boston University has one of the most impressive collections of personal papers of any American institution. Among its holdings are the papers of Bette Davis, Douglas Fairbanks, Jr., Angela Lansbury, Roddy McDowall, Joan Fontaine, Rise Stevens, Gene Kelly, Anne Revere, Jean Pierre Aumont, Don Siegel, Everett Chambers, Sam Shepherd, Jesse Lasky, Arthur Marx, Robert Parrish, Ben Piazza, Norman Reilly Raine, Robert Redford, Kate Smith, Leonard Spigelgass, Sam Wanamaker, Robert Benchley, Daniel Fuchs, Claude Rains, Basil Rathbone, Michael Blankfort, Norman Corwin,

Maya Deren, Helen Deutsch, Fred and Adele Astaire, Nora Kaye, Herbert
Ross, Charles Higham, Glenda Jackson, Nunnally Johnson, Martyn Green,
John Lahr, Anthony Newley, Frank S. Nugent, Harry Richman, Irene
Mayer Selznick, Mary Astor, Robert Carson, Ilka Chase, Albert Maltz,
Curt Siodmak, and Edward Wagenknecht.

Brandeis University
Brandeis University Library
415 South Street
Waltham, MA 02154
(617) 647–2514

The Arthur Laurents Collection here includes play and film scripts, along
with correspondence and notes.

Brandeis University
National Center for Jewish Film
Lown Building 102
Waltham, MA 02254
(617) 899–7044

The Center was established in 1976 "to gather, preserve, and disseminate
film material relevant to the Jewish experience." It serves as a center where
scholars may view relevant films and conduct research, and among its
holdings are prints of *Romance of a Jewess* (1908), *His People* (1925), *Surrender*
(1927), and many Yiddish features.

Harvard Business School
Baker Library
Soldiers Field
Boston, MA 02163
(617) 495–6395

The Library has some of the business records, from 1894 to 1921, of the
pioneering film organization Raff and Gammon.

Harvard College Library
Harvard Theatre Collection
Cambridge, MA 02138
(617) 495–1000

One of the best known theatre collections in the world, the Harvard
Theatre Collection contains more than 3 million programs and playbills,

650,000 photographs and 15,000 costume and scenic designs. Among the collections here are those of Alix Jeffry, Angus McBean, Robert Gould Shaw, Otis Skinner, Edward B. Sheldon, Thomas Wood, William Como, Norma McLain Stoop, and the *Mademoiselle* entertainment files from 1964 to 1980. Russian drama is covered by the H. W. L. Dana Collection, and there are some 12,000 portrait photographs of film stars in the William E. Thayer Collection. Major film collections here include the complete set of designs by Jean Hugo for Carl Dreyer's *The Passion of Joan of Arc* and Roger Furse's set designs for Olivier's *Hamlet*.

Smith College
Werner Josten Library of the Performing Arts
Mendenhall Center
Northampton, MA 01063
(413) 584–2700

The emphasis is on music, but there are also collections relating to theatre and dance.

Tufts University
Murrow Center of Public Diplomacy
Medford, MA 02155
(617) 628–5000

The Center has the personal papers, books, films, tapes, and other material of the man after whom it is named, Edward R. Murrow.

Michigan _____

American Museum of Magic
107 East Michigan
Marshall, MI 49068
(616) 781–7666

The Museum's Irving Desfor Collection contains more than 40,000 items, including books, correspondence, photographs, clippings, and periodicals.

Detroit Institute of the Arts
5200 Woodward Avenue
Detroit, MI 48202
(313) 833–7926

The Institute is the repository for the Paul McPharlin Collection of Puppetry and Theater.

E. Azalia Hackley Collection
5201 Woodward Avenue
Detroit, MI 48202
(313) 833–1465

A collection of books, photographs, posters, music, and records documenting Black contributions to theatre, music, dance, film, radio, and television from the eighteenth century to the present.

Michigan State University Library
East Lansing, MI 48824
(517) 355–3770

The Library houses the Florence Vandamm collection of photographs of Broadway productions and performers from 1925 to 1958.

Wayne State University
Archives of Labor and Urban Affairs
Detroit, MI 48202
(313) 577–4024

There are some film-related items, as well as films and videotapes, in various collections relating to American labor.

Minnesota

Blackwood Hall Memorial Library
Blackwood Hall Theatre Collection
205 Fourth Avenue
Albert Lea, MN 56007

Papers here include those of Ralph Forbes and Joan Fontaine.

Guthrie Theatre Foundation Library
725 Vineland Place
Minneapolis, MN 55403
(612) 347-1133

The Library maintains a collection of plays, books, photographs, and other items, together with a complete set of programs for the Guthrie Theatre.

University of Minnesota
Eric Sevareid Journalism Library
121 Murphy Hall
206 Church Street S.E.
Minneapolis, MN 55455
(612) 625-7892

As its name suggest, the Library holds the papers of the veteran radio and television journalist.

University of Minnesota Library
Performing Arts Archives
Minneapolis, MN 55455
(612) 373–7271

The Performing Arts Archives have built up a collection of photographs, posters and documents relating to the history of theatre and film in Minnesota.

Missouri

Missouri Historical Society
Jefferson Memorial Building
Forest Park
St. Louis, MO 63112
(314) 361–1424

The Society has a collection of 10,000 theatre programs from 1817 to the present.

University of Missouri-Kansas City
General Library
5100 Rockhill Road
Kansas City, MO 64110
(816) 276–1531

The Library houses a collection of film scores composed by Leith Stevens.

New Hampshire _____

Dartmouth College
Dartmouth College Library
Hanover, NH 03755
(603) 646–1110

Established in 1937 by Walter Wanger as a memorial to the Hollywood producer, the Irving Thalberg Script Collection at Dartmouth includes more than 2,000 items.

New Jersey _____

David Sarnoff Research Center and Library
RCA Corporation
Princeton, NJ 08540
(609) 734–7608

The Center is a major resource for the study of the technological development of radio and television. In 1987, the Center was transferred from the General Electric Company to SRI International, a non-profit research and consulting organization.

Edison National Historic Site
Box 126
Orange, NJ 07051
(201) 736–5050

The Edison National Historic Site, the location of the inventor's laboratory, contains documentation on all of Thomas Edison's activities, including the records of the Edison Film Company.

Fort Lee Public Library
320 Main Street
Fort Lee, NJ 07024
(201) 592–3614

The Library collects documentation, including photographs, relating to early film making in the Fort Lee area.

Princeton University
William Seymour Theatre Collection
Firestone Library
Princeton, NJ 08544
(609) 452–3223

Founded in 1936 by the children of William Seymour, the Collection includes Seymour's own papers documenting his career in the theatre, as well as the papers of Fanny Davenport, Otto Kahn, Max Gordon, Trans-Witmark, Edwin Forrest, Allan Tate, and others, together with the archives of the McCarter Theatre, the Triangle Club, and the Theatre Intime of Princeton University. The business papers from the New York office of Warner Bros. are also housed in the Collection. For more information on the last, see Jensen, Mary Ann. "The Warner Brothers Collection at Princeton University Library." In *Performing Arts Resources*, edited by Ginnine Cocuzza and Barbara Naomi Cohen-Stratyner, vol. 10, 16. New York: Theatre Library Association, 1985.

New Mexico _____

Albuquerque Public Library
501 Copper NW
Albuquerque, NM 87102
(505) 766–7722

The Library houses some clippings relating to film making in New Mexico and also has an index to *TV Guide* from 1961 to the present.

New Mexico State Records Center and Archives
Historical Film Collection
404 Montezuma
Santa Fe, NM 87503
(505) 827–8860

The collection consists of both paper documentation and films relating to early film making in New Mexico.

New York _____

Alix Jeffry
71 West 10 Street
New York, NY 10011
(212) 982–1835

A commercial photographic library, Alix Jeffry holds more than 50,000 items on off-Broadway theatre in New York from 1952 onwards. Included here are photographs from the plays of Edward Albee and musical productions at New York City Center.

American Mime, Inc. Library
61 Fourth Avenue
New York, NY 10003
(212) 677–9276

American Mime was founded in 1970 and collects materials documenting the history of mime theatre in the United States.

American Museum of Natural History
Central Park West at 79 Street
New York, NY 10024
(212) 873–1300

The Museum houses a large collection of ethnological films.

Anthology Film Archives
80 Wooster Street
New York, NY 10012
(212) 226–0010

An organization devoted to the study and preservation of independent film and video, Anthology Film Archives maintain a study collection and a reference library, consisting of books, periodicals, clippings, posters, artwork, and other material. A listing of films in its collection, as of 1975, was published in *The Essential Cinema: Essays on the Films in the Collection of Anthology Film Archives*, edited by P. Adams Sitney. New York: New York University Press, 1975.

Archives of Experimental Art
351 West 30 Street
New York, NY 10001
(212) 564–5989

Among the avant-garde art subjects included here are theatre, music and dance.

Astoria Motion Picture and Television Foundation
34–31 35th Street
Astoria, NY 11106
(212) 784–4520

Created in 1977 and intended to become a major museum of film and television arts, Astoria is primarily concerned with the history of film making in New York and its environs. It holds collections of still photographs, lobby cards, and posters, as well as costumes donated by the Eaves Costume Company and the papers of director Frank Tuttle. Back issues of its journal are deposited at Astoria by the Society of Motion Picture and Television Engineers, for distribution to professional organizations and educational institutions.

Astoria also created an oral history program to document the activities of the studio in which it is housed, and among those interviewed are George Cukor, Allan Dwan, Colleen Moore, Reuben Mamoulian, George Folsey, Constance Binney, Louise Brooks, Joe Smith, Jetta Goudal, Madge Kennedy, Lois Wilson, and Rudy Vallee.

Bettman Archive
136 East 57 Street
New York, NY 10022
(212) 758–0362

The Bettman Archive is a commercial photographic archive with considerable holdings relating to the performing arts, including a large film stills library collected by publicist John Springer.

Cayuga Museum of History and Art
203 Genesee Street
Auburn, NY 13021
(315) 253–8051

The Museum is housed, in part, in the Theodore W. Case Laboratory, and it was Case, together with E. I. Sponable, who experimented with early sound-on-film. The Museum's collection contains materials relating to their work.

Columbia University Library
Department of Special Collections
116 Street and Broadway
New York, NY 10027
(212) 280–2271

Among the film-related collections at Columbia are copies of documentary film maker Robert Flaherty's correspondence from the twenties through the forties and the archives of the Twentieth Century–Fox Research Department, documenting the development of sound-on-film, Grandeur, and CinemaScope. A major theatrical collection consists of the sketches of designer Joseph Urban. A major radio resource is the papers of Edwin Armstrong, the inventor of FM Radio. Other collections are the papers of Erik Barnouw and scripts from the TV series "The Defenders."

Columbia University
Oral History Research Office
Box 20, Butler Library
116 Street and Broadway
New York, NY 10027
(212) 280–2273

The University has compiled a unique collection of transcribed and indexed oral histories covering the development of the performing arts in the twentieth century. Among the subjects interviewed are Dana Andrews, Richard Barthelmess, James Cagney, Frank Capra, Bosley Crowther, Melvyn Douglas, Gracie Fields, Albert Hackett, Buster Keaton, Harold Lloyd, Anita Loos, Myrna Loy, Frances Marion, Conrad Nagel, Mary Pickford, Otto Preminger, Jean Renoir, David O. Selznick, King Vidor, and Adolph Zukor. For more information, see *The Oral History Collection of Columbia University*, edited by Elizabeth B. Mason and Louis M. Starr. New York: Oral History Research Office, 1973.

Cornell University Libraries
Department of Manuscripts and University Archives
101 Olin Research Library
Ithaca, NY 14853
(607) 256–3530

The papers of Irene Castle here include materials relating to both her careers on stage and as a film actress, together with items on the early motion picture industry in Ithaca.

Dell Publishing Company Inc. Library
One Dag Hammarskjold Plaza
New York, NY 10017
(212) 605–3000

There are considerable files here of photographs and biographies of film and television personalities.

Educational Film Library Association
45 John Street, Suite 301
New York, NY 10038
(212) 227–5599

The Educational Film Library Association is a valuable resource for the study of films intended for the educational market and for non-theatrical distribution. Its Library includes books, periodicals, film catalogs, and a card index to more than 50,000 films.

Hispanic Society of America Library
613 West 155 Street
New York, NY 10032
(212) 926-2234

The Society collects documentation on Spanish theatre from the seventeenth century to the present.

Hofstra University
Hofstra University Library
1000 Fulton Avenue
Hempstead
Long Island, NY 11550
(516) 560-5940

Hofstra University houses a small collection of materials relating to dramatist and director Harold Pinter, including taped interviews.

International Museum of Photography at
George Eastman House
900 East Avenue
Rochester, NY 14607
(716) 271-3361

The George Eastman House maintains a research library covering both film and photography, as well as a major collection of film and pre-cinema equipment. It has more than 1 million still photographs, a major portion of which consist of stills from First National and Warner Bros. films. The film collection is relatively small—slightly more than 5,000 titles—but all of the films are important to the history of the motion picture, and George Eastman House is particularly rich in the productions of Metro-Goldwyn-Mayer, Thomas H. Ince, Cecil B. DeMille, and William S. Hart.

International Theatre Institute of the United States, Inc.
220 West 42 Street
New York, NY 10036
(212) 944-1490

Founded in 1970, the Institute has a collection of theatre-related books, periodicals, plays, programs, photographs, and other items from 142 countries.

Jewish Museum
National Jewish Archive of Broadcasting
1109 Fifth Avenue
New York, NY 10128
(212) 860–1886

Founded in 1981, the Archive is concerned with the acquisition and preservation of news, religious, public affairs, and entertainment programs whose subject matter is of interest to the Jewish community. It also maintains a library of books, press releases, and clippings.

The Museum of Broadcasting
1 East 53 Street
New York, NY 10022
(212) 752–4690

Founded in 1976 by William S. Paley, the Museum of Broadcasting houses a unique collection of radio and television programs available for research. More than 10,000 videotapes of television shows, dating back to 1939, are held by the Museum, with the nucleus of its radio holdings being the NBC Radio Archive, consisting of 175,000 discs dating from 1927 to 1969. The Museum also maintains a small library of books and periodicals, as well as a collection of radio scripts. The now out-of-date *Catalog of the Museum of Broadcasting: The History of American Broadcasting as Documented by the Programs in the Radio and Television Collection* was published by Arno Press (New York) in 1981.

For more information, see "What the Dumbwaiter Saw" by Mary V. Ahern, pp. 84–88, "Using the Museum of Broadcasting's Catalogue" by Douglas Gibbons, pp. 89–90, and "Creating an Exhibition at the Museum of Broadcasting" by Judith E. Schwartz, pp. 91–93. In *Performing Arts Resources*, edited by Mary C. Henderson. New York: Theatre Library Association, 1980.

Museum of Modern Art
Film Department
11 West 53 Street
New York, NY 10020
(212) 708–9613

The Museum of Modern Art has one of the finest collections of films, from a quality viewpoint, in the world, and many of its films are available for viewing in its Film Study Center. The Center also contains clippings files on individual films and personalities. Film-related books may be found in the Museum's Library, and more than 3 million stills are available for study and purchase of copies in the Film Stills Archive. The major paper collection here is devoted to D. W. Griffith (including scrapbooks and correspondence), but there are also collections relating to Thomas H. Ince and Robert Flaherty, as well as the collections of Barnet Braverman and Merritt Crawford and assorted Edison Company scripts. Also of interest is a poster collection, a script collection, documents relating to the censorship of Russian silent films in New York, the Artkino Collection of scripts and other items on Soviet Cinema, Cinema 16 program notes from 1947 to 1963, and papers relating to Carl Lerner's work as an editor and director.

Museum of the City of New York
Theatre and Music Collection
103 Street and Fifth Avenue
New York, NY 10028
(212) 534–1672

The Museum is rich in artifacts relating to the history of theatre in New York, with special collections relating to William A. Brady, Lillian Gish, Helen Hayes, Charles Frohman, Daniel Frohman, Howard Dietz, Jenny Lind, Alfred Lunt and Lynn Fontanne, Mary Martin, Ethel Merman, Kate Claxton, and others. It also has an impressive collection of stage designs and costumes.

National Association of Broadcasters
Television Information Office
745 Fifth Avenue
New York, NY 10022
(212) 759–6800

The Television Information Office was founded in 1959 to provide "a two-way bridge of understanding between the television industry and its many publics." It offers a library and information service and publishes a number of bibliographies.

Neighborhood Playhouse School of the Theatre
Irene Lewisohn Library
340 East 54 Street
New York, NY 10022
(212) 688–3770

A general theatre collection of books, periodicals, photographs, clippings, and other material.

New York Historical Society
170 Central Park West
New York, NY 10024
(212) 873–3400

The Society houses a considerable amount of material relating to theatre in New York, as well as surrounding states. Its manuscript holdings include the correspondence of William Dunlap, John Thomson Ford, Ruth Draper, Annie Elizabeth Burke, and Charles Walter Couldock. Other rare items include the autobiography of Mrs. Tom Thumb, the diaries of Gertrude Kellogg, Voltaire's manuscript of *Charlot on La Comtesse de Givry*, and the Phineas Taylor Barnum circus collection.

New York Public Library
Schomberg Center for Research in Black Culture
515 Lenox Avenue
New York, NY 10037
(212) 862–4000

This major center for Black research includes materials relating to the history of Blacks in theatre and film.

The New York Public Library
Theatre Collection of the Performing Arts Research Center
Lincoln Center
111 Amsterdam Avenue
New York, NY 10023
(212) 930–0800

The New York Public Library at Lincoln Center, with its files covering every aspect of the performing arts, is, arguably, the major resource center for research in the United States. The history of American theatre from 1870 to 1920 is covered in the 800 volumes of clippings, programs, letters, and photographs in the Robinson Locke Collection. Other major theatrical collections include those of David Belasco, George Becks, Hiram Stead, and the Dramatists Guild of the Authors League. Two major collections of theatrical photographs are those of Carl Van Vechten and the Vandamn Studio.

Major film-related items include the still books of Universal Pictures, the scrapbooks and still books of Inspiration Pictures, scrapbooks from the Capitol Theatre, New York, and Loews, Inc., and the scrapbooks of the Kalem Company. The Library also has a superior collection of film periodicals, dating back to 1907. Television and radio are also covered in script collections, including a complete set for the Hallmark television specials.

Among the papers in the Library are those of the Chamberlain and Lyman Brown Theatrical Agency, the Society of American Magicians, the Lambs Club, Brooks Atkinson, Katharine Cornell, Helen Hayes, Klaw and Erlanger, Maurice Evans, Edward Albee, Leland Hayward, Sophie Tucker, Clifford Odets, Montgomery Clift, Paul Muni, John Golden, Jean Dalrymple, and the Group Theatre.

New York State Archives
Albany, NY 12230
(518) 474–1195

Between 1921 and 1965, all films to be screened publicly in the State of New York had to be passed by the censorship board. Its records are now on deposit with the Archives and include what is unquestionably the largest collection of screenplays—more than 50,000—in any institution. For more information, see Johnpoll, Bernard K. "A Treasure Trove for Film Scholars." In *The New York Times*, 15 June 1980: D15–D16.

New York University
Fales Library
70 Washington Square South
New York, NY 10012
(212) 598–3756

There are a number of theatrical collections here, including the papers of Elizabeth Robins, Erich Maria Remarque, Sholom Secunda, and Richard Schechner and the Performance Group. The Library also holds items relating to the dramatization of works by Charles Dickens, productions of *Alice in Wonderland*, playscripts and promptbooks of Arthur Wing Pinero, the Oscar Cargill Photograph Collection, letters of George Bernard Shaw relating to the theatre, and the archives of the Provincetown Players.

New York University
Robert F. Wagner Labor Archives
The Tamiment Institute Library
70 Washington Square South
New York, NY 10012
(212) 598–3708 or 598–7754

The Robert F. Wagner Labor Archives began the acquisition of performing arts collections in 1981 with the historical records of the Actors Equity

Association (contracts, legal files, photographs, and correspondence). The Archives also hold the records of the American Guild of Variety Artists, Equity Library Theatre and the Actors Fund of America. As part of the New York City Labor Records Survey Project, the Archives conduct site surveys of the historical records of New York–based labor unions and organizations associated with the performing arts.

For more information, see Nelson, Steve. "Performing Arts Collection at the Robert F. Wagner Labor Archives." In *Performing Arts Resources*, edited by Ginnine Cocuzza and Barbara Naomi Cohen-Stratyner, vol. 10. New York: Theatre Library Association, 1985.

Penguin Photo Collection
663 Fifth Avenue
New York, NY 10022
(212) 758–7328

A commercial library, specializing in the history of popular entertainment—theatre, film, radio, television, music, and dance—from 1870 to the present.

Pierpont Morgan Library
29 East 36 Street
New York, NY 10016
(212) 685–0008

Aside from a valuable collection of letters from prominent theatrical actors and writers, the Pierpont Morgan Library houses the Mary Flagler Cary Music Collection and the Gilbert & Sullivan Collection (consisting of manuscripts, posters, programs, and other items).

Players Club
The Walter Hampden-Edwin Booth Theatre Collection and
Library
16 Gramercy Park
New York, NY 10003
(212) 228–7610

The basis for the Library is the papers of Edwin Booth and Walter Hampden. The John Mulholland Magic Collection is an important resource for study on the subject. Burlesque sketches may be found in the Chuck Callahan Collection. Tapes of the Players Pipe Nights are housed in the Library, with the subjects including Maurice Chevalier, James Cagney, Fredric March, Danny Kaye, Jack Benny, Marlene Dietrich, and Rex Harrison. Additional collections include the papers of the Union Square Theatre, Tallulah Bankhead, George M. Cohan, Maurice Evans, Max Gordon, Newman Levy, Robert B. Mantell, and Muriel Kirkland.

Show Business Association Library
1501 Broadway
New York, NY 10036
(212) 354–7600

This Library houses a collection of 14,000 books primarily relating to entertainment and the law.

Shubert Archive
149 West 45 Street
New York, NY 10036
(212) 944–3895

Housed in the Lyceum Theatre, the Shubert Archive was established in 1976 to house the records of the Shubert Organization. It includes legal and financial records from 1900 to 1979, music from 1900 to 1940, playscripts from 1900, costume designs from 1900 to 1940, technical drawings from 1900 to 1970, architectural plans from 1900 to 1970, and press and publicity materials from 1900 to the present.

State University of New York at Albany
Film and Television Documentation Center
1400 Washington Avenue
Albany, NY 12222
(518) 455–6238

Aside from publishing the quarterly *Film Literature Index*, the Center houses a data base of information invaluable for film research.

SUNY at Binghamton
Glenn G. Bartle Library
Vestal Parkway East
Binghamton, NY 13901
(607) 777–2194

The Library houses not only the papers of actress Tillie Losch, but, more importantly, the Max Reinhardt Collection, consisting of more than 250,000 items (including personal papers, Reinhardt's personal library, and scene and costume designs).

SUNY at Stony Brook
Department of Special Collections and University Archives
Stony Brook, NY 11794–3323
(516) 246–3615

Among the drama-related collections here are Chilean theatre pamphlets and the Performing Arts Foundation Collection.

Syracuse University
E. S. Bird Library
Syracuse, NY 13210
(315) 423–2585

The Library specializes in collections relating to mass communication, and among the major resources here are the papers of actor Ed Begley, radio writer and personality Gertrude Berg, television reporter Irving R. Levine, and radio and television personality Fulton Lewis. The Library also holds scripts, interviews, notes, and recordings from Norman Corwin and scripts and recordings from Mike Wallace. The *Television Quarterly* Collection consists of correspondence, reports and manuscripts submitted to the journal. The Library also houses the papers, including scores, of two major film composers, Miklos Rozsa and Franz Waxman.

J. Walter Thompson Co. Archives
466 Lexington Avenue
New York, NY 10017
(212) 210–7000

The archives of this advertising agency include documentation on a number of popular radio and television series, such as "Kraft Music Hall," "Lux

Radio Theatre," and "The Chase and Sanborn Hour with Edgar Bergen and Charlie McCarthy." For more information, see Swank, Cynthia G. "Performing Arts on Madison Avenue." In *Performing Arts Resources*, edited by Ginnine Cocuzza and Barbara Naomi Cohen-Stratyner, vol. 10, 23–25. New York: Theatre Library Association, 1985.

Yivo Institute for Jewish Research
1048 Fifth Avenue
New York, NY 10028
(212) 535–6700

The Institute collects documentation on Jewish theatre from the nineteenth century to the present.

North Carolina _____

University of North Carolina at Chapel Hill
Institute of Outdoor Drama
Chapel Hill, NC 27514
(919) 962–1328

    The Institute is concerned with both the historical and current aspects of outdoor theatre production and collects documentation on the subject.

Ohio

Bowling Green State University
Center for Study of Popular Culture
Popular Culture Center
Bowling Green, OH 43402
(419) 372–2981

The leading resource center for the study of popular culture as it relates to motion pictures, radio and television, Bowling Green State University collects items as varied as matchbook covers, book illustrations, comic books, mail order catalogs, programs, cigarette cards, and cigar bands.

Cincinnati and Hamilton County Public Library
800 Vine Street
Cincinnati, OH 45202
(513) 369–7954

Aside from considerable music holdings, the Library has more than 16,000 theatre programs and other drama-related documentation.

Cleveland Public Library
325 Superior Avenue
Cleveland, OH 44114–1271
(216) 623–2881

Aside from holdings of some 20,000 theatre programs and 130,000 still photographs, the Cleveland Public Library also houses the Barrett W. Clark Collection, the William F. McDermott Memorial Theatre Collection, and the W. Ward Marsh Cinema Archives.

Kent State University
Kent State University Libraries
Kent, OH 44242
(216) 672–2270

Among the collections here are the papers of actress Lois Wilson, film professor Gerald Mast, the archives of *After Dark* magazine, and the personal library of prolific film book writer James Robert Parish.

Ohio Historical Society
1–71 and 17th Avenue
Columbus, OH 43211
(614) 466–1500

The Society houses the records of the Ohio Censorship Board from 1913 to 1954, plus additional censorship materials from other states and countries.

Ohio State University
Theatre Research Institute
1089 Drake Union
1849 Cannon Drive
Columbus, OH 43210
(614) 422–6614

Collections here relate to the Sadler's Wells Theatre in London, the Austrian Burgtheater, local Ohio theatre, and European theatre from the fifteenth century. The Institute also publishes the annual *Theatre Studies*.

Ohio State University
Ohio State University Libraries
Milton Caniff Research Room
242 West 18th Avenue, Room 147
Columbus, OH 43210
(614) 422–8747

The Room is named in honor of the noted cartoonist Milton Caniff, whose papers were donated to the University in 1973. Also included here are more than 100,000 film posters and still photographs from 1939 to 1964, donated by Philip Sills.

Ottawa Institute
Irene Holm Memorial Library
1465 Osborn Drive
Columbus, OH 43221
(614) 486–5028

Of interest here are the more than 3,000 audio tapes in the Arthur Lindner Memorial Collection of Historic Radio Broadcasts.

University of Dayton
Roesch Library
300 College Park Avenue
Dayton, OH 45469
(513) 229–4221

The Library holds the papers of the Victory Theatre.

Oklahoma _____

Claremore Junior College
Lynn Riggs Memorial
Claremore, OK 74017
(918) 341–7510

The papers of the author of *Green Grow the Lilacs*, upon which *Oklahoma!* is based, are housed in his home town junior college.

Tom Mix Museum
721 North Delaware
Dewey, OK 74029
(918) 534–1555

A major collection of memorabilia, including a $15,000 silver-mounted saddle, is gathered together in the community where cowboy star Tom Mix was once town marshall.

Will Rogers Memorial
Claremore, OK 74017
(918) 341–0719

The Oklahoma home of Will Rogers now houses his personal papers, scripts, photographs, memorabilia, and scrapbooks, as well as the scrapbooks of Fred Stone and Homer Croy. Microfilm copies of the various scrapbooks are also on deposit with the University Library, Oklahoma University, Stillwater, OK 74074.

Oregon _____

Oregon Historical Society
1230 West Park Avenue
Portland, OR 97205
(503) 222–1741

The Society collects documentation, including film, on the history of the motion picture as it pertains to Oregon.

Portland Art Museum
Northwest Film Study Center
Southwest Park and Madison Streets
Portland, OR 97205
(503) 226–2811

The Center houses a collection of clippings, posters, and oral history interviews.

University of Oregon
University of Oregon Library
Eugene, OR 97403
(503) 686–3069

Among the collections here are those of Harry Behn, Lowell Brentano, Richard J. Collins, John Thomas Flynn, Vance Joseph Hoyt, Margaret Lynch, Willy Pogany, Fred Steiner, Axel Stordahl, Charles Marquis Warren, and Ruth Cornwall Woodman.

Pennsylvania _____

Allentown College
John Y. Kohl American Theatre Collection
Center Valley, PA 18034
(215) 202–1100

Founded in 1965, this collection consists primarily of American playbills and theatre programs.

Charlotte Cushman Club
239 S. Camac Street
Philadelphia, PA 19107
(215) 735–4676

Founded in 1907, the Club houses the scrapbooks, programs, clippings, and memorabilia of America's first major, native-born actress.

Franklin and Marshall College
Shadek-Fackenthal Library
Lancaster, PA 17604
(717) 291–4216

The Library houses the papers, including scripts, correspondence, notes, and photographs, of television and film director Franklin J. Schaffner. Also here is the Alexander Corbett Collection of Theatre Memorabilia, consisting of more than 600 photographs and letters.

The Free Library of Philadelphia
The Theatre Collection
Logan Circle
Philadelphia, PA 19103
(215) 686–5427

The Theatre Collection has the primary responsibility for acquiring every-thing relating to entertainment in Philadelphia and Pennsylvania. It contains books, magazines, playbills, programs, posters, photographs, and other me-morabilia covering theatre, motion pictures, minstrels, vaudeville, circus, radio, and television. The Library's Philadelphia Theatre Index lists every major production in the city since 1855 and partially indexes the collection of local playbills, dating back to 1803. Early film companies, such as the Philadelphia-based Lubin Company, are represented in the Collection by more than 30,000 still photographs. Circus programs and route books date back to 1900, and there are minstrel programs as early as 1860. Most significant are the manuscripts from Philadelphia's Dumont's Minstrels. The Collection is currently the second largest theatre collection in an American public library.

Friends Free Library
Germantown Friends Meeting
5418 Germantown Avenue
Philadelphia, PA 19144
(215) 438–6013

The Library's holdings include 250 scrapbooks comprising the Irvin Poly Theater History of Philadelphia from 1904 to 1965.

Historical Society of Pennsylvania
1300 Locust Street
Philadelphia, PA 19107
(215) 732–6200

The Society holds the Ellis Paxson Oberholtzer Papers on motion picture censorship.

Pennsylvania State University
Fred Lewis Pattee Library
University Park, PA 16802
(814) 865–0401

Aside from a good general collection of books, pamphlets, and periodicals relating to the performing arts, the Library also holds some items relating to screen adaptations of the author's works in the John O'Hara Collection as well as the archives of American Theatre Lighting, documenting the development of stage lighting in the twentieth century. For more information on the latter, see Allison, William. "The Penn State Archives of American Theatre Lighting including Century Lighting and Century Strand Control System Drawings; 1950–1970." In *Performing Arts Resources*, edited by Ginnine Cocuzza and Barbara Naomi Cohen-Stratyner, vol. 10, 40–48. New York: Theatre Library Association, 1985.

University of Pennsylvania
Annenberg School of Communications Library
3620 Walnut Street
Philadelphia, PA 19104
(215) 898–7027

The Library is dedicated to the study of communications, including television. It maintains a large television script collection, as well as the Sol Worth Ethnographic Film Archive.

University of Pennsylvania
Van Pelt Library
3420 Walnut Street
Philadelphia, PA 19104
(215) 898–7091

The University houses a number of performing arts–related collections, the pride of which consists of the papers of Theodore Dreiser. Additionally, the University has a fine collection of plays in manuscript form.

University of Pittsburgh
Curtis Theatre Collection
363 Hillman Library
Pittsburgh, PA 15260
(412) 624–4428

The Collection is primarily devoted to theatre in New York and Pittsburgh and includes some 500,000 programs, books, scrapbooks, plays, and clippings. The Merriman Scrapbook Collection consists of 142 scrapbooks on theatre in Pittsburgh and New York from 1880 to 1941.

Rhode Island _____

Providence Public Library
150 Empire Street
Providence, RI 02903
(401) 521-7722

Housed here is the library of a practicing magician, John H. Percival.

Rhode Island Historical Society
121 Hope Street
Providence, RI 02906
(401) 331-8575

The Society holds considerable materials relating to local theatre and film history, along with an unpublished history of the circus in Providence.

South Carolina _____

South Carolina Historical Society
Fireproof Building
100 Meeting Street
Charleston, SC 29401
(803) 723–3225

The Society holds the papers, plays, and screenplays of DuBose Heyward.

Tennessee _____

Country Music Foundation
Library and Media Center
700 16th Avenue South
Nashville, TN 37203
(615) 256–7008

Founded in 1964, the Foundation maintains a library of videotapes and 16mm films.

Memphis State University
John Willard Brister Library
Memphis, TN 38152
(901) 454–2210

Memphis State University holds the papers of two major figures in twentieth-century theatre history, Edward Gordon Craig and Jed Harris.

Memphis State University Libraries
Radio Program History Collection
Brister Library Learning Media Center
Memphis, TN 38152
(901) 454–2001

The collection consists of more than 3,000 radio broadcasts dating from the twenties through the sixties.

University of Tennessee Library
Knoxville, TN 37916
(615) 974–4480

The Library houses the papers of one of the University's better known alumni and a major film director, Clarence Brown. The collection includes scripts, still photographs, awards, lobby cards, scrapbooks, and correspondence. The Library's Music Division holds the collection of opera star, and occasional film actress, Grace Moore.

Vanderbilt University
Jean and Alexander Heard Library
419 21st Avenue South
Nashville, TN 37240–0007
(615) 322–2807

The Library has the Francis Robinson Theatre Collection, which consists primarily of books.

Vanderbilt University Library
Vanderbilt Television News Archive
419 21st Avenue South
Nashville, TN 37203
(615) 322–2927

The Vanderbilt Television News Archive consists of a videotape collection of the evening broadcasts of the three major networks since August 5, 1968. These broadcasts are indexed from descriptive abstracts, and such indexes are published monthly in *Television News Index and Abstracts*. In addition to the news broadcasts, the Archive tapes additional items, such as presidential addresses and press conferences, political conventions, and Senate and House hearings (such as the Watergate hearings).

Texas

Dallas Public Library
1515 Young Street
Dallas, TX 75201
(214) 749–4236

The Library is rich in materials on Dallas theatre history, including documentation on the W. E. Hill Theatre, Margo Jones Theatre, Dallas Theater Center, and Dallas Little Theatre.

Marion Koogler McNay Art Museum
6000 N. New Braunfels Avenue
San Antonio, TX 78209
(512) 824–5368

The Museum maintains a collection on the history of costume and scenic design in the theatre.

San Antonio Public Library
210 W. Market Street
San Antonio, TX 78205
(512) 299–7810

The Harry Hertzberg circus collection here is considered one of the country's finest.

Southern Methodist University
Fondren Library
McCord Theater Collection
Dallas, TX 75275
(214) 692–2400

The Collection includes materials on vaudeville, films, radio, television, dance, and opera. There is material here on the Corsicana Opera House and the Dallas Little Theatre. Southern Methodist University also sponsors an oral history project on the performing arts, and those interviewed include Steve Allen, Fred Astaire, Mel Blanc, Yul Brynner, Rosemary Clooney, Imogene Coca, George Cukor, Nanette Fabray, Will Geer, Bonita Granville, Edith Head, Gene Kelly, Pinky Lee, Virginia Mayo, Lloyd Nolan, Pat O'Brien, David Raksin, Robert Stack, Mel Torme, Rudy Vallee, King Vidor, Slavko Vorkapich, and Adolph Zukor.

University of Houston
Anderson Memorial Library
University Park Campus
Houston, TX 77004
(713) 749–2725

The University houses the papers of major Broadway producer Cheryl Crawford.

University of Texas at Austin
Humanities Research Center
Box 7219
Austin, TX 78713
(512) 471–9122

The best known of the collections here is that of David O. Selznick, containing more than 1 million items, including correspondence, scripts, still photographs, legal documents, scrapbooks, awards, costume and set designs, and memos. Other major collections include those of Maurice Zolotow, Gloria Swanson, Ernest Lehman, Norman Bel Geddes, Alfred Junge, King Vidor, Edward Carrick, John Gassner, along with the Stanley Marcus Collection of Sicilian Marionettes and the Joe E. Ward Collection of Circus Memorabilia. The Hoblitzelle Interstate Circuit Music Collection includes thousands of items used to accompany silent films. The Center also possesses a good collection of books, periodicals, still photographs, films, videotapes, scripts, clippings, and posters.

Utah

Brigham Young University
Archives of Recorded Sound
5030 Harold B. Lee Library
Provo, UT 84602
(801) 378–6373

As its name suggests, this is a collection of tape recordings—more than 45,000—of film soundtracks and radio broadcasts.

Brigham Young University
Harold B. Lee Library
Provo, UT 84602
(801) 378–1211

The Arts and Communications Archives of the Library house a number of film-related collections, most notable of which are the papers of producer-director Cecil B. DeMille. The Library also houses the papers of Howard Hawks, Andy Devine, Dean Jagger, Victor Milner, Doty-Dayton Productions, National Association of Theatre Owners, Sunset Films, Irwin A. Bazelon, and Mark Evans. Mary Astor's scrapbook on *Brigham Young* (1940) is here, as are the papers of a number of writers on film subjects, including Carol Easton, George Fenin, Arthur Lennig, Cynthia Lindsay, Richard Nelson, and Lawrence Suid.

Utah Historical Society
603 East South Temple
Salt Lake City, UT 84102
(801) 533–5755

The Society collects documentation on film making in Utah and films by Utah residents or about their state.

Virginia _____

George Mason University
Center for Government, Society and the Arts
4400 University Drive
Fairfax, VA 22030
(703) 323–2546

Formerly known as the Federal Theatre Research Center, this unit of George Mason University houses the archives of the Federal Theatre Project of the W.P.A. (Works Progress Administration) from 1935 to 1939, including theatre and radio scripts, clippings, and posters. The Center also maintains an oral history program with participants in the W. P. A. Arts Projects. For more information, see "Federal Theatre Project Records at George Mason University." In *Performing Arts Resources*, edited by Mary C. Henderson, vol. 6. New York: Theatre Library Association, 1980.

University of Virginia
Alderman Library
Charlottesville, VA 22901
(804) 924–3026

The Library's William Faulkner Collection includes materials relating to screen adaptations of Faulkner's works as well as scripts by Faulkner himself.

Washington _____

Gonzaga University
Crosby Library
East 502 Boone Avenue
Spokane, WA 99258
(509) 328–4220

Opened in 1957 as a gift from Gonzaga University's best-known alumnus, Harry L. "Bing" Crosby, the Crosby Library contains the entertainer's memorabilia, as well as personal papers, scripts, music scores and other items.

University of Washington
Drama Library
145 Hutchinson Hall
Seattle, WA 98195
(206) 543–4148

Founded in 1931, the Library maintains a major collection of plays, books, and periodicals covering all aspects of theatrical history. Among its collections are the records of the Allied Arts of Seattle, the Barrett H. Clark collection of playscripts, the scripts and records of the University of Washington Drama School, and the records and scripts of the Seattle Repertory Playhouse.

Wisconsin

American Players Theatre, Inc. Library
Route 3
Spring Green, WI 53588
(608) 588–7401

Founded in 1977, the American Players Theatre maintains a library of books, playbills, clippings, and architectural drawings on the theatre, with particular emphasis on English, French, German, Greek, and Russian drama.

Circus World Museum Library and Research Center
Baraboo, WI 53913
(608) 356–8341

A collection of circus memorabilia, including photographs, posters, prints, films, clippings, route books, leaflets, and other items dating from 1890 to the present.

Milwaukee Public Library
814 W. Wisconsin Avenue
Milwaukee, WI 53233
(414) 278–3000

Aside from a quantity of film posters, the Milwaukee Public Library possesses a major collection of items relating to the Pabst German Theatre Company's work in Milwaukee.

University of Wisconsin
Polk Library
800 Algoma Boulevard
Oshkosh, WI 54901
(414) 424–3333

The Library houses the collection—books, films, tapes, and other items— of critic and film maker Pare Lorentz.

Wisconsin Center for Film and Theater Research
816 State Street
Madison, WI 53706
(608) 262–0585

With more than 500 collections on the subject, the Wisconsin Center for Film and Theater Research is one of the most important institutions for study of the dramatic arts in the United States. In addition to paper collections, it also houses 16mm prints of films produced by Warner Bros., RKO, and Monogram.

Among the collections here are those of Harry and Roy Aitken, Robert Altman, Pandro S. Berman, Herbert Biberman and Gale Sondergaard, Claude H. Binyon, Marc Blitzstein, Daniel L. Blum, David Brinkley, Vera Caspary, Gilbert Cates, Paddy Chayefsky, Shirley Clarke, Fred Coe, John Cromwell, Emile De Antonio, I. A. L. Diamond, Kirk Douglas, Melvyn Douglas, Michael Douglas, John Frankenheimer, Ketti Frings, Zona Gale, Ernest Gold, Frances Goodrich and Albert Hackett, Moss Hart and Kitty Carlisle, Edith Head, Nat Hiken, Hal Holbrook, Chet Huntley, Dorothy Jeakins, Norman Jewison, Albert R. Johnson, Hans V. Kaltenborn, Hal Kanter, Walter and Jean Kerr, Howard E. Koch, Millard Lampel, Howard Lindsay and Russel Crouse, Louis P. Lochner, Joseph McBride, Terrence McNally, Albert Maltz, Fredric March, Winston Miller, Newton N. Minow, Walter Mirisch, Agnes Moorehead, National Broadcasting Company (1921–1969), National Educational Television (1951–1970), Edwin H. Newman, Samuel B. Ornitz, Paul Osborn, Howard Rodman, Reginald Rose, Jerome Ross, Dore Schary, George Seaton, Sidney Sheldon, Herman E. Shumlin, Howard K. Smith, Stephen Sondheim, Ed Sullivan, David Susskind, Dalton Trumbo, United Artists Corporation, Clifton M. Utley, Dale Wasserman, and Nedrick Young.

For more information, see *Sources for Mass Communications, Film and Theater Research: A Guide.* Madison, Wis: State Historical Society of Wisconsin, 1982.

Wyoming _____

University of Wyoming
Division of Rare Books and Special Collections
Box 3334
Laramie, WY 82071
(307) 766–4114

Among the many dramatic-arts-related collections here are the papers of Ed Begley, Wally Cox, Louis de Rochemont, Dorothy Devore, Clifton Fadiman, Bryan Foy, Ethel Grandin, Rose Hobart, Harry Horner, Rochelle Hudson, Michael and Fay Kanin, Babe London, David Manners, Ozzie and Harriet Nelson, Eleanor Powell, Ray Smallwood, and George K. Spoor.

Who's Who

The following section provides biographical information on some 200 leading academics, archivists, critics, historians, librarians, and scholars, involved in theatre, film, radio, and television.

Each entry includes a description of the individual's professional status, followed by date and place of birth, educational background, current, and sometimes former, affiliation, major accomplishments, a list of published books and pamphlets, and a mailing address.

ABEL, RICHARD, professor of English. b. August 20, 1941, Canton, Ohio; B.A., Utah State University; M.A., University of Southern California; Ph.D., University of Southern California; professor of English, Drake University. Publication: *French Cinema: The First Wave, 1915–1929*, 1984. 1514 29th Street, Des Moines, IA 50311.

ADLER, RENATA, film critic and writer. b. October 19, 1938, Milan, Italy; A.B., Bryn Mawr College, 1959; M.A., Harvard University, 1960; Dd.E.S., Sorbonne, 1961; J.D., Yale University, 1979; staff writer, *The New Yorker*, 1962 to present; film critic, *The New York Times*, 1968–1969. Publications: *A Year in the Dark*, 1970; *Toward a Radical Middle*, 1970; *Speedboat*, 1976; *Pitch Dark*, 1983. The New Yorker, 25 West 43 Street, New York, NY 10036.

ALLEN, NANCY, librarian. b. October 4, 1950, Illinois; B.A., University of Illinois at Urbana, 1972; M.S., University of Illinois at Urbana, 1973;

communications librarian, University of Illinois at Urbana, 1978–1984; assistant director for public services, Wayne State University Libraries, 1984–1986; assistant director for services, Wayne State University Libraries, 1986 to present; editor, *Cinema Librarians' Newsletter*, 1977–1986. Publications: *Film Study Collections: A Guide to Their Development and Use*, 1979; *Annotated Catalog of Unpublished Film and Television Scripts in the University of Illinois Library at Urbana-Champaign*, with Robert Carringer, 1983. Purdy Library, Wayne State University, Detroit, MI 48202.

ALLEN, ROBERT C., professor of film and media studies. b. August 13, 1950, Charlotte, North Carolina; B.A., Davidson College; M.A., University of Iowa; Ph.D., University of Iowa; associate professor, Department of Radio, Television, and Motion Pictures, University of North Carolina, 1984 to present; series editor, with James Carey and Daniel Leab, *American Broadcasting in History and Culture*; associate editor, *Cinema Journal*, 1984 to present. Publications: *Vaudeville and Film, 1895–1915*, 1980; *Speaking of Soap Operas*, 1985; *Film History: Theory and Practice*, with Douglas Gomery, 1985. 3481 Hope Valley Road, Durham, NC 27707.

ALPERT, HOLLIS, film and theatre critic. b. September 24, 1918, Herkimer, New York; founding editor, *American Film*, 1975–1981. Selected Publications: *The Dreams and the Dreamers*, 1962; *The Barrymores*, 1964; *Playboy's Sex in the Cinema*, with Arthur Knight, 1970; *Playboy's Sex in the Cinema 2*, with Arthur Knight, 1972; *Playboy's Sex in the Cinema 3*, with Arthur Knight, 1973; *The Actor's Life*, editor, 1978; *Burton*, 1986; *Fellini, a Life*, 1986. Box 1006, Shelter Island, NY 11964.

ANDREW, DUDLEY, professor of film. b. July 28, 1945, Evansville, Indiana; B.A., University of Notre Dame, 1967; M.F.A., Columbia University; Ph.D., University of Iowa; visiting professor, University of California at Los Angeles, 1977–1978; professor and head of film studies, University of Iowa department of communication studies, 1981 to present; member editorial boards, *Wide Angle*, *UFVA Journal*, *Quarterly Review of Film Studies*, *Film Criticism*. Publications: *The Major Film Theories*, 1978; *André Bazin*, 1978; *Kenji Mizoguchi: A Guide to References and Resources*, 1981; *Concepts in Film Theory*, 1984; *Film in the Aura of Art*, 1984. 1157 Court Street, Iowa City, IA 52240.

APPLEBAUM, STANLEY, editor. b. September 11, 1934, New York; B.A., Brooklyn College, 1954; M.A., Yale, 1955; editor-in-chief, Dover Publications, Inc. Selected Publications: *The Movies: A Picture Quiz Book*, with Hayward Cirker, 1972; *The Hollywood Musical: A Picture Quiz Book*, 1974; *Show Songs from "The Black Crook" to "The Red Mill"*, 1974; *Silent Movies: A Picture Quiz Book*, 1974; *The New York Stage: Famous Productions in Photographs*, 1976; *Advertising Woodcuts from the Nineteenth-Century Stage*,

1977; *Stars of the American Musical Theatre in Historic Photographs*, with JamesCamner, 1981; *Great Actors and Actresses of the American Stage in Historic Photographs*, 1983. Dover Publications, Inc., 180 Varick Street, New York, NY 10014.

ARLEN, MICHAEL J., writer and television critic. b. December 9, 1930, London, England; TV critic, *The New Yorker*, 1957 to present. Selected Publications: *Living-Room War*, 1969; *Exiles*, 1970; *The View from Highway 1*, 1976; *The Camera Age*, 1981. The New Yorker, 25 West 43 Street, New York, NY 10036.

BALIO, TINO, professor of film. b. November 12, 1937, Albion, Michigan; B.A., Wabash College, 1959; M.A., Indiana University, 1961; Ph.D., Indiana University, 1964; professor of film, department of communication arts, University of Wisconsin at Madison. Publications: *United Artists: The Company Built by the Stars*, 1975; *The American Film Industry*, 1976. Department of Communication Arts, University of Wisconsin, Madison, WI 53706.

BALL, ROBERT HAMILTON, professor of English. b. May 21, 1902, New York; A.B., Princeton University, 1923; A.M., Princeton University, 1924; Ph.D., Princeton University, 1928; professor emeritus of English, Queens College, City University of New York, 1971 to present. Publications: *The Amazing Career of Sir Giles Overreach*, 1939; *The Plays of Henry C. DeMille*, editor, 1941; *A Short View of Elizabethan Drama*, with Thomas Parrott, 1943, 1960; *Theatre Language*, with Walter Bowman, 1961; *Shakespeare on Silent Film*, 1968. 11 North Washington Street, Port Washington, NY 11050.

BARNES, CLIVE, theatre and dance critic. b. May 13, 1927, London, England; B.A., Oxford University, 1951; dance and drama critic, *The New York Times*, 1967–1978; drama critic, *New York Post*, 1978 to present. Publications: *Ballet in Britain since the War*, 1953; *Frederick Ashton and His Ballets*, 1961; *Ballet Here and Now*, 1961; *Dance Scene, U.S.A.*, 1967; *Inside American Ballet Theatre*, 1977; *Nureyev*, editor, 1983. New York Post, 210 South Street, New York, NY 10002.

BARNOUW, ERIK, professor of dramatic arts. b. June 23, 1908, The Hague, Netherlands; joined Columbia University as a faculty member, 1946; chief, motion picture, broadcasting, and recorded sound division, Library of Congress, 1978–1981; professor emeritus of dramatic arts, Columbia University. Publications: *Mass Communication: Television, Radio, Film, Press*, 1956; *Indian Film*, with S. Krishnaswamy, 1963; *A Tower in Babel*, 1966; *The Golden Web*, 1968; *The Image Empire*, 1970; *Documentary: A History of the Nonfiction Film*, 1974; *Tube of Plenty: The Evolution of Amer-*

ican Television, 1975; *The Sponsor: Notes on a Modern Potentate*, 1978; *The Magician and the Cinema*, 1981. 39 Claremont Avenue, New York, NY 10027.

BASINGER, JEANINE, professor of film. b. February 3, 1936, Ravenden, Arkansas; B.S., South Dakota State University, 1957; M.S., South Dakota State University, 1959; associate professor of film studies, Wesleyan University, 1980–1984; professor of film studies, Wesleyan University, 1984 to present; trustee, American Film Institute, 1979 to present; curator and founder, Wesleyan Cinema Archives. Publications: *Working with Kazan*, co-editor, 1973; *Shirley Temple*, 1975; *Gene Kelly*, 1976; *Lana Turner*, 1977; *Anthony Mann: A Critical Analysis*, 1979; *Anatomy of a Genre: World War II Combat Films*, 1986; *The It's a Wonderful Life Book*, 1986. 133 Lincoln Street, Middletown, CT 06457.

BEHLMER, RUDY, writer, lecturer, director, producer. b. October 13, 1926, San Francisco; B.A., Los Angeles City College and Pasadena Playhouse College, 1950; executive producer-director, KCOP-TV, Los Angeles, 1960–1962; vice-president, Leo Burnett, Inc., 1963–1984; lecturer in film studies, Art Center College of Design, Pasadena, 1966 to present; lecturer in film studies, California State University, Northridge, 1984 to present. Selected Publications: *The Films of Errol Flynn*, with Tony Thomas and Clifford McCarty, 1969; *Memo from David O. Selznick*, 1972; *Hollywood's Hollywood*, with Tony Thomas, 1975; *America's Favorite Movies*, 1982; *Inside Warner Bros.*, 1985. 3972 Tropical Drive, Studio City, CA 91604.

BELL, GEOFFREY, film maker. b. August 18, 1909, San Francisco; former military career in U.S. coast guard; producer of the following documentary films on motion picture history: *The Movies Go West, The First (Motion) Picture Show, Those Daring Young Film Makers.* Publication: *The Golden Gate and the Silver Screen*, 1984. 1007 Sutter Street, No. 406, San Francisco, CA 94109.

BELTON, JOHN, film professor. b. June 18, 1945, Cleveland, Ohio; B.A., Columbia University, 1967; M.A., Harvard University, 1969; Ph.D., Harvard University, 1975; assistant professor, Columbia University, 1978–1986; visiting professor, Yale University, 1986. Publications: *Hollywood Professionals: Howard Hawks, Frank Borzage and Edgar G. Ulmer*, 1974; *Robert Mitchum*, 1976; *Cinema Stylists*, 1983; *Film Sound: Theory and Practice*, with Elisabeth Weis, 1985. 243 Baltic Street, Brooklyn, NY 11201.

BENTLEY, ERIC, writer and playwright. b. September 14, 1916, England; B.A., Oxford University, 1938; Ph.D., Yale University, 1941; drama critic, *The New Republic*, 1952–1956; Brander Matthews professor of dramatic literature, Columbia University, 1953–1969; Katharine Cornell professor of theatre, SUNY, Buffalo, 1974 to present. Selected Publications: *A Century of Hero-Worship*, 1944; *Bernard Shaw*, 1947; *In Search of Theatre*, 1953; *The Life of the Drama*, 1964; *Are You Now?*, 1972; *Brecht Commentaries*, 1981; *Before Brecht*, 1985; *The Pirandello Commentaries*, 1986. 194 Riverside Drive, New York, NY 10025.

BERGREEN, LAWRENCE, writer. b. February 4, 1950, New York; A.B., Harvard University, 1972. Publications: *Look Now, Pay Later: The Rise of Network Broadcasting*, 1980; *James Agee: A Life*, 1984. c/o Peter Lampack Agency, 551 Fifth Avenue, New York, NY 10017.

BONDANELLA, PETER, professor of Italian Studies and Italian Cinema. b. December 20, 1943, Pinehurst, North Carolina; A.B., Davidson College, 1966; M.A., Stanford University, 1967; Ph.D., University of Oregon, 1970; professor, center for Italian Studies, Indiana University, 1972 to present. Publications: *Federico Fellini: Essays in Criticism*, 1978; *Italian Cinema: From NeoRealism to the Present*, 1983; *Federico Fellini, Director: "La Strada"*, 1987; *The Eternal City: Roman Images in the Modern World*, 1987. Center for Italian Studies, 642 Ballantine Hall, Indiana University, Bloomington, IN 47405.

BORDMAN, GERALD, writer. b. September 18, 1931, Philadelphia; B.A., Lafayette College, 1952; M.A., University of Pennsylvania, 1953; Ph.D., University of Pennsylvania, 1957. Publications: *American Musical Theatre: A Chronicle*, 1978; *Jerome Kern: His Life and Music*, 1980; *American Operetta: From "HMS Pinafore" to "Sweeney Todd"*, 1981; *Day To Be Happy, Years To Be Sad*, 1982; *American Musical Comedy: From "Adonis" to "Dreamgirls,"* 1982. c/o Oxford University Press, 200 Madison Avenue, New York, NY 10016.

BORDWELL, DAVID, film professor. b. July 23, 1947, Rochester, New York; B.A., State University of New York at Albany, 1969; M.A., University of Iowa, 1972; Ph.D., University of Iowa, 1974; professor and director of the Center for Film and Theater Research, Department of Communication Arts, University of Wisconsin at Madison. Publications: *Film Guide to "La Passion de Jeanne d'Arc,"* 1973; *Film Art: An Introduction*, with Kristin Thompson, 1979; *French Impressionist Cinema: Film Culture, Film Theory, Film Style*, 1980; *The Films of Carl-Theodor Dreyer*, 1981; *The Classical Hollywood Cinema*, with Janet Staiger and Kristin Thompson, 1985; *Narration in the Fiction Film*, 1985. 544 South Owen Drive, Madison, WI 53711.

BOWSER, EILEEN, film archivist. b. January 18, 1928, Columbia Station, Ohio; B.A., Marietta College, 1950; M.A., University of North Carolina, 1953; staff member, department of film, Museum of Modern Art, 1954 to present; curator, department of film, Museum of Modern Art, 1976 to present. Publications: *Carl Dreyer*, 1964; *D. W. Griffith*, with Iris Barry,

1965; *Film Notes*, editor, 1969; *Biograph Bulletins 1908–1912*, editor, 1973; *The Movies*, with Richard Griffith and Arthur Mayer, 1981. Museum of Modern Art, 11 West 53 Street, New York, NY 10019.

BOYUM, JOY GOULD, film critic. b. December 8, 1934, New York; B.A., Barnard College; M.A., New York University; Ph.D., New York University; film critic, *The Wall Street Journal*, 1971–1983; film critic, *Glamour*; professor of English and communication arts, New York University. Publications: *Film as Film: Critical Approaches to Film Art*, 1970; *Double Exposure: Fiction into Film*, 1985. 45 Remsen Street, Brooklyn Heights, NY 11201.

BRAUDY, LEO, professor of English. b. June 11, 1941, Philadelphia; B.A., Swarthmore College, 1963; M.A., Yale University, 1964; Ph.D., Yale University, 1967; professor of English, University of Southern California, 1983 to present. Publications: *Narrative Form in History and Fiction*, 1970; *Jean Renoir: The World of His Films*, 1972; *Norman Mailer: A Collection of Critical Essays*, editor, 1972; *Focus on Shoot the Piano Player*, editor, 1972; *World in a Frame: What We See in Films*, 1977; *Great Film Directors*, co-editor with Morris Dickstein, 1978. Department of English, University of Southern California, Los Angeles, CA 90089.

BROOKS, TIM, writer. b. April 18, 1942, New Hampshire; B.A., Dartmouth College, 1964; M.S., Syracuse University, 1969; staff member, NBC-TV, 1976 to present and currently director of program research; adjunct professor, C. W. Post College, 1980 to present. Publications: *The Complete Directory to Prime Time Network TV Shows, 1946-Present*, with Earle Marsh, 1979; *TV in the '60s*, with Earle Marsh, 1985; *TV's Greatest Hits*, with Earle Marsh, 1985. NBC-TV, 30 Rockefeller Plaza, New York, NY 10020.

BROWN, LES, writer and television critic. b. December 20, 1928, Indiana Harbor, Indiana; B.A., Roosevelt University, 1950; editor, radio-TV department, *The New York Times*, 1965–1973; radio-TV correspondent, *The New York Times*, 1973–1980; editor-in-chief, *Channels of Communication*, 1980 to present. Publications: *Television: The Business behind the Box*, 1971; *Electric Media*, 1973; *New York Times Encyclopedia of Television*, 1977; *Keeping Your Eye on Television*, 1979; *Les Brown's Encyclopedia of Television*, 1982. 131 North Chatsworth Avenue, Larchmont, NY 10538.

BROWNE, NICHOLAS, professor of film and television. b. October 26, 1944; B.A., Williams College, 1966; M.A., University of Chicago, 1970; Ed.D., Harvard University, 1976; professor, department of theater, film and television, University of California at Los Angeles, 1984 to present; chairman, film and television studies committee, department of theater, film and television, University of California at Los Angeles, 1984 to present.

Publications: *The Rhetoric of Filmic Narration*, 1982; *Western Film Studies: Contempory Film Theory*, 1984; *The Politics of Representation: Perspectives from Cahiers du Cinéma*, 1969–1972. Department of Theater, Film and Television, University of California, 405 Hilgard Avenue, Los Angeles, CA 90024.

BUKALSKI, PETER J., professor of film and theater. b. June 5, 1941, Milwaukee, Wisconsin; B.A., University of Wisconsin at Milwaukee, 1963; M.A., University of Wisconsin at Milwaukee, 1964; M.F.A., University of California at Los Angeles, 1966; Ph.D., Ohio State University, 1975; professor of film and theater and dean, school of fine arts and communications, Southern Illinois University at Edwardsville. Publication: *Film Research*, 1972. Box 1770, Southern Illinois University, Edwardsville, IL 62026.

CALLENBACH, ERNEST, editor and writer. b. April 3, 1929, Pennsylvania; Ph.B., University of Chicago, 1949; M.A. University of Chicago, 1953; founder and editor, *Film Quarterly*, 1958 to present; editor of science books, University of California Press, 1970 to present; editor of natural history guides series, University of California Press, 1975 to present. Publications: *Our Modern Art: The Movies*, 1955; *Living Poor with Style*, 1972; *Ecotopia*, 1975; *The Art of Friendship*, with Christine Leefeldt, 1979; *Ecotopia Emerging*, 1981; *The Ecotopian Encyclopedia for the 80s: A Survival Guide*, 1981; *A Citizen Legislature*, with Michael Phillips, 1985; *Humphrey the Wayward Whale*, with Christine Leefeldt, 1985. University of California Press, 2120 Berkeley Way, Berkeley, CA 94720.

CANBY, VINCENT, film critic. b. July 27, 1924, Chicago; B.A., Dartmouth College, 1947; film critic, *The New York Times*, 1969 to present. The New York Times, 229 West 43 Street, New York, NY 10036.

CARD, JAMES, film archivist and historian. b. October 25, 1915, Cleveland, Ohio; A.B., Western Reserve University, 1938; member of staff, International Museum of Photography at George Eastman House, 1948–1977; member of faculty, University of Rochester, 1966 to present; recipient of Society of Motion Picture and Television Engineers Eastman Kodak Gold Metal, 1977; co-founder, Telluride Film Festival and World Film Festival, Montreal. P.O. Box 616, East Rochester, NY 14445.

CARRINGER, ROBERT L., professor of film. b. May 12, 1941, Knoxville, Tennessee; M.A., Johns Hopkins University, 1964; Ph.D., Indiana University, 1970; professor of English and film, University of Illinois at Urbana-Champaign; member editorial boards, *Cinema Journal* and *Quarterly Review of Film Studies*. Publications: *Ernst Lubitsch*, with Barry Sabath, 1978; *The Jazz Singer*, 1979; *Citizen Kane*, Laserdisc CAV Edition, 1984; *The Making of "Citi-*

zen Kane", 1985; *The Magnificent Ambersons*, Laserdisc CAV Edition, 1986. 608 S. Wright Street, University of Illinois, Urbana, IL 61801.

CASTY, ALAN HOWARD, professor of English. b. April 6, 1929, Chicago; B.A., University of California at Los Angeles, 1950; M.A., University of California at Los Angeles, 1956; Ph.D., University of California at Los Angeles, 1956; professor, department of English, Santa Monica College, 1956 to present. Selected Publications: *Robert Rossen*, 1967; *Mass Media and Mass Man*, 1968, 1973; *The Films of Robert Rossen*, 1969; *The Dramatic Art of the Film*, 1971; *Development of the Film: An Interpretive History*, 1973. 3646 Manderville Canyon Road, Los Angeles, CA 90049.

CHACH, MARYANN, performing arts archivist and librarian. b. August 31, 1949, Jersey City, New Jersey; B.A., New York University, 1971; M.L.S., Columbia University, 1973; M.A., New York University, 1977; director of information services, Educational Film Library Association, 1977–1983; associate editor, *Sightlines*, 1977–1983; editor, *EFLA Bulletin*, 1980–1983; assistant director, library services, The Museum of Broadcasting, 1983–1984; performing arts librarian, Bobst Library, New York University, 1984–1987; librarian, Shubert Archive, 1987 to present. Publication: *Film Library Administration Bibliography*, 1978. 121 West 72 Street, Apt. 2A, New York, NY 10023.

CHAMPLIN, CHARLES, critic. b. March 23, 1926, Hammondsport, New York; A.B., Harvard, 1948; arts editor and critic at large, *Los Angeles Times*. Publication: *The Movies Grow Up*, 1980. Los Angeles Times, Times Mirror Square, Los Angeles, CA 90053.

COE, RICHARD L., drama critic. b. November 8, 1914, New York; radio editor and assistant drama critic, *The Washington Post*, 1938–1942; writer-editor, Middle East edition of *Stars and Stripes*, 1943–1946; drama critic and amusements editor, *The Washington Post*, 1946–1979; drama critic emeritus, *The Washington Post*, 1979 to present; commentator, WRC-TV, 1969–1976; "The Richard L. Coe Award" was established by the New Playwrights' Theater of Washington, DC in 1980. 2101 Connecticut Avenue, NW, Washington, DC 20008.

COLEMAN, MARY JANE, film festival director. b. November 25, 1923, Portsmouth, Virginia; founder and director, Sinking Creek Film Celebration, 1970 to present; visiting lecturer, Tusculum College. 1250 Old Shiloh Road, Greeneville, TN 37743.

COOK, DAVID A., professor of film. b. August 14, 1945, St. Louis, Missouri; B.A., University of Maryland, 1967; Ph.D., University of Virginia,

1971; assistant professor, Purdue University, 1971–1973; assistant professor, Emory University, 1973–1977; associate professor, Emory University, 1977–1985; professor, Emory University, 1986 to present; director, film studies program and film acquisitions, theater and film studies department, Emory University, 1986 to present. Publication: *A History of Narrative Film*, 1981. Department of English, Emory University, Atlanta, GA 30322.

COOPER, T. G., professor of theatre. b. August 14, 1939; B.F.A., Howard University; M.A., University of Miami; professor of drama, Howard University, 1962 to present; also playwright, theatre producer and director. Publications: *Obeah: God of Voodoo*, 1978; *Onstage in America*, 1984. Department of Drama, College of Fine Arts, Howard University, Washington, DC 20001.

CORLISS, RICHARD, film critic. b. March 6, 1944, Philadelphia; B.S., St. Joseph's College, 1965; M.F.A., Columbia University, 1967; editor, *Film Comment*, 1970 to present; associate editor, *Time*, 1980–1985; senior writer, *Time*, 1985 to present. Publications: *The Hollywood Screenwriters*, editor, 1972; *Talking Pictures: Screenwriters in the American Cinema 1927–1973*, 1974; *Greta Garbo*, 1974. Time, Time & Life Building, New York, NY 10020.

CRAFTON, DONALD C., professor of film. b. April 26, 1947, Springfield, Missouri; B.A., University of Michigan; M.A., University of Iowa; M.A., Yale University; Ph.D., Yale University; professor of film, University of Wisconsin at Madison. Publication: *Before Mickey: The Animated Film 1898–1928*, 1982. Department of Communication Arts, 6110 Vilas Hall, University of Wisconsin, Madison, WI 53706.

CRAIN, WILLIAM H., theatre curator. b. July 19, 1917, Victoria, Texas; B.A., 1940; M.A., 1943; B.F.A., 1947; M.F.A., 1949; curator, Harry Ransom Humanities Research Center, University of Texas at Austin, 1965 to present. Publication: *Some Personal Notes and Manuscripts of John Gassner: A Checklist of the Holographics and Typescript Materials in the John Gassner Collection of Dramatic Criticism*, 1968. P.O. Drawer 7219, Austin, TX 78713–7219.

CRIPPS, THOMAS, professor of history. b. September 17, 1932, Baltimore, Maryland; B.S., Towson State College, 1954; M.A., University of Maryland, 1957; Ph.D., University of Maryland, 1967; professor of history, Morgan State University, 1961 to present. Publications: *Slow Fade to Black: The Negro in American Film, 1900–1942*, 1977; *Black Film as Genre*, 1978; *The Green Pastures*, editor, 1979. 1714 Bolton Street, Baltimore, MD 21217.

CRIST, JUDITH, film critic. b. May 22, 1922, New York; A.B., Hunter College, 1941; M.Sc., Columbia University, 1945; adjunct professor, graduate school of journalism, Columbia University, 1964 to present; film critic, *TV Guide,* 1965 to present. Publications: *The Private Eye, the Cowboy and the Very Naked Lady,* 1968; *Judith Crist's TV Guide to the Movies,* 1974; *Take 22: Moviemakers on Moviemaking,* 1984. 180 Riverside Drive, New York, NY 10024.

CROCE, ARLENE, writer and dance critic. b. May 5, 1934, Providence, Rhode Island; B.A., Barnard College, 1955; founder and editor, *Ballet Review,* 1965–1978; dance critic, *The New Yorker,* 1973 to present. Publications: *The Fred Astaire & Ginger Rogers Book,* 1972; *Afterimages,* 1977; *Going to the Dance,* 1982. The New Yorker, 25 West 43 Street, New York, NY 10036.

CROWDUS, GARY, editor and film distributor. b. January 2, 1945, Lexington, Kentucky; B.F.A., New York University's Institute of Film and Television, 1969; founding editor of *Cineaste,* 1967 to present; vice-president and general manager, The Cinema Guild. 116 St. Marks Place, Apt. 8, New York, NY 10009.

CURTIS, JAMES R., writer and biographer. b. November 16, 1953, Los Angeles; B.A., California State University, Fullerton, 1979. Publications: *Between Flops,* 1982; *James Whale,* 1982. 1051-C North Bradford Avenue, Placentia, CA 92670.

DARDIS, TOM, professor of English. b. August 19, 1927, New York; A.B., New York University; M.A. and M.Phil., Columbia University; Ph.D., Columbia University; professor of English, John Jay University, CUNY. Publications: *Some Time in the Sun,* 1976; *Keaton,* 1979; *Harold Lloyd,* 1983. 2500 Johnson Avenue, New York, NY 10463.

DICK, BERNARD, professor of English. b. November 25, 1935, Scranton, Pennsylvania; B.A., University of Scranton, 1957; M.A., Fordham University, 1960; Ph.D., Fordham University, 1962; professor of English and comparative literature, Fairleigh Dickinson University, 1973 to present. Selected Publications: *A Critical Study of Gore Vidal,* 1974; *Anatomy of Film,* 1978; *Billy Wilder,* 1980; *Hellman in Hollywood,* 1982; *Joseph L. Mankiewicz,* 1983; *The Star-Spangled Screen,* 1985. 989 Wilson Avenue, Teaneck, NJ 07666.

DUCEY, MAXINE FLECKNER, archivist. b. April 13, 1950, Oak Park, Illinois; B.A., New York University, 1975; M.A., University of Wisconsin at Madison, 1985; associate film archivist, Wisconsin Center for Film and Theater Research 1976–1979; director of the film archive, Wisconsin Center for Film and Theater Research, 1979 to present. Publication: *Women's History Resources at the State Historical Society of Wisconsin*, 1982. 2906 Lakeland Avenue, Madison, WI 53704.

DUCLOW, GERALDINE, performing arts librarian. b. September 20, 1946, Chicago; B.A., DePaul University, 1967; M.L.S., Rosary College, 1968; curator, theatre collection, Free Library of Philadelphia, 1972 to present. Theatre Collection, Free Library of Philadelphia, Logan Circle, Philadelphia, PA 19103.

EBERT, ROGER, film critic. b. June 18, 1942, Urbana, Illinois; B.S., University of Illinois, 1964; film critic, *Chicago Sun-Times*, 1967 to present; lecturer in film criticism, University of Chicago, 1969 to present; co-host, "Sneak Previews," 1977–1982; co-host, "At the Movies," 1982–1986; co-host, "Siskel & Ebert & the Movies," 1986 to present. Publications: *An Illini Century*, 1967; *Beyond the Valley of the Dolls*, 1970; *Beyond Narrative: The Future of the Feature Film*, 1978; *A Kiss Is Still a Kiss*, 1984; *Roger Ebert's Movie Home Companion*, 1985; *The Perfect London Walk*, with Daniel Curley, 1986. 401 North Wabash Avenue, Chicago, IL 60611.

ELLIS, JACK C., professor of film, radio and television. b. July 9, 1922, Joliet, Illinois; M.A., University of Chicago, 1948; Ed.D., Columbia University, 1955; professor of film, Northwestern University, 1956 to present; chairman, department of radio, television, and film, 1980–1985; editor *Cinema Journal*, 1976–1982; advisory editor, *Cinema Journal*, 1982 to present. Publications: *A History of Film*, 1979; *The Film Book Bibliography 1940–1975*, with Charles Derry and Sharon Kern, 1979; *Cinema Examined*, with Richard Dyer MacCann, 1982; *John Grierson: A Guide to References and Resources*, 1986. Department of Radio, Television, and Film School, Northwestern University, Evanston, IL 60201.

ESSERT, GARY, administrator. b. 1938, Oakland, California; founder and director/chief executive officer, Los Angeles International Film Exposition (Filmex), 1971–1983; artistic director, the American Cinematheque; producer, "The Movies," 1975; producer, "An Evening with Elizabeth Taylor," 1981. 3612 Woodhill Canyon Road, Studio City, CA. 91604.

EVERSON, WILLIAM K., film historian. b. April 8, 1929, Yeovil, England; film history instructor, New York University and The New School for Social Research. Selected Publications: *The Western*, with George N. Fenin, 1962, 1973; *The American Movie*, 1963; *The Bad Guys*, 1964; *The Films of Laurel & Hardy*, 1967; *The Art of W. C. Fields*, 1967; *The Detective in Film*, 1972; *Classics of the Horror Film*, 1974; *American Silent Film*, 1978; *Love in the Film*, 1979. 118 West 79 Street, New York, NY 10024.

FEINGOLD, MICHAEL, theatre critic. b. May 5, 1945, Chicago; B.A., Columbia University, 1966; M.F.A., Yale School of Drama, 1970; drama critic, *The Village Voice,* 1971 to present; lecturer, dramatic writing program, New York University, 1985 to present; translations of many plays by Bertolt Brecht and others. The Village Voice, 842 Broadway, New York, NY 10003.

FELL, JOHN L., professor of film. b. September 19, 1927, Westfield, New Jersey; A.B., Hamilton College, 1950; M.A., New York University, 1954; Ph.D., New York University, 1958; professor emeritus, film department, San Francisco State University. Publications: *Film and the Narrative Tradition,* 1974; *Film: An Introduction,* 1976; *A History of Films,* 1977; *Film before Griffith,* editor, 1983. 10 Palm Court, Larkspur, CA 94939.

FIELDING, RAYMOND, professor of film and television. b. January 3, 1931, Brockton, Massachusetts; B.A., University of California at Los Angeles, 1953; M.A., University of California at Los Angeles, 1956; Ph.D., University of Southern California, 1961; associate professor, division of radio-television-film, department of speech and drama, University of Iowa, 1966–1969; professor of communication, department of radio-television-film, school of communication and theater, Temple University, 1969–1978; professor of communication, school of communications, University of Houston, 1978 to present; president, Society for Cinema Studies, 1972–1974; president, University Film and Video Association, 1967–1968; trustee, American Film Institute, 1973–1979; president, University Film and Video Foundation, 1985 to present. Publications: *The Technique of Special Effects Cinematography,* 1965; *A Technological History of Motion Pictures and Television,* 1967; *The American Newsreel, 1911–1967,* 1972; *The March of Time, 1935–1951,* 1978. School of Communication, University of Houston, University Park, Houston, TX 77004.

FINCH, CHRISTOPHER, writer. b. 1939, United Kingdom. Selected Publications: *The Art of Walt Disney,* 1973; *Rainbow: The Stormy Life of Judy Garland,* 1975; *Walt Disney's America,* 1978; *Gone Hollywood,* with Linda Rosenkrantz, 1979; *On Muppets and Men: The Making of the Muppet Show,* 1981. c/o Clarke Literary Agency, 28 East 95 Street, New York, NY 10028.

FORDIN, HUGH, writer. b. December 17, 1935, New York; B.S., Syracuse University, 1957. Publications: *Film TV Daily Yearbook 1970,* editor, 1970; *The New Jerome Kern Song Book,* editor, 1974; *That's Entertainment Song Book,* editor, 1974; *Hollywood's Royal Family: The Freed Unit,* 1974; *Oscar Hammerstein II: Getting To Know Him,* 1976; *The World of Entertainment: Hollywood's Greatest Musicals,* 1976. c/o Curtis Brown Ltd., 575 Madison Avenue, New York, NY 10022.

FRENCH, WARREN G., professor of American Studies and editor. b. January 26, 1922, Philadelphia; B.A., University of Pennsylvania, 1943; M.A., University of Texas at Austin, 1948; Ph.D., University of Texas at Austin, 1954; D.H.L., Ohio University, 1985; editor, Twayne "Filmmakers" series, 1977–1987. Selected Publications: *A Filmguide to "The Grapes of Wrath,"* 1973; *The South and Film,* 1982. 23 Beechwood Road, Uplands, Swansea, Wales, SA2 OHL, United Kingdom.

GALLAGHER, TAG, professor of film. b. June 17, 1943, Philadelphia; A.B., Georgetown University, 1968; M.A., New York University, 1971; Ph.D., Columbia University, 1978; assistant professor, division of liberal arts, Babson College, 1979–1984. Publication: *John Ford: The Man and His Work,* 1986. 1253 Tanager Lane, West Chester, PA 19382.

GEDULD, HARRY M., professor of film. b. March 3, 1931, London, England; B.A., Sheffield University, 1953; M.A., Sheffield University, 1954; Ph.D., University of London, 1961; professor of comparative literature/film studies, Indiana University, 1961 to present; film reviewer, *The Humanist,* 1967 to present; series editor, "Film Focus" (Prentice-Hall), "Filmguides" (Indiana University Press) and "The Literature of Detection and Mystery" (Arno Press). Selected Publications: *Film Makers on Film Making,* 1967; *Sergei Eisenstein and Upton Sinclair: The Making and Unmaking of "Que Viva Mexico!,"* with Ronald Gottesman, 1970; *Focus on D. W. Griffith,* 1971; *Authors on Film,* 1972; *The Birth of the Talkies,* 1975; *The Girl in the Hairy Paw,* with Ronald Gottesman, 1976; *Charlie Chaplin's Own Story,* 1985. Department of Comparative Literature, Ballantine 402, Indiana University, Bloomington, IN 47405.

GELMIS, JOSEPH S., film critic. b. September 28, 1935, Brooklyn, New York; B.A., Brooklyn College, 1956; M.A., Columbia University, 1960; former faculty member, SUNY at Stony Brook; critic and editor, *Newsday.* Publication: *The Film Director as Superstar,* 1970. c/o Newsday, 780 Third Avenue, New York, NY 10017.

GELTZER, GEORGE, film researcher. b. September 20, 1921, Bronx, New York; active in visual aids on silent films at the New York School for the Deaf, 1935–1940; contributor of many career articles to *Films in Review, Quirk's Reviews* and others. 102–30 66th Road, Forest Hills, NY 11375.

GILL, BRENDAN, writer and theatre critic. b. October 4, 1914, Hartford, Connecticut; A.B., Yale University, 1936; film critic, *The New Yorker,* 1960–1967; drama critic, *The New Yorker,* 1968–1987. Selected Publications: *Cole,* with Robert Kimball, 1971; *Tallulah,* 1972; *Happy Times,* 1973. The New Yorker, 25 West 43 Street, New York, NY 10036.

GILL, SAMUEL A., archivist. b. April 24, 1946, Sterling, Kansas; B.A., University of Kansas, 1968; Certificate, Archives-Library Institute, Ohio Historical Society, 1974; author, "The Funnymen" column, *8mm Collector*, 1964–1967; archivist, Academy of Motion Picture Arts and Sciences, 1975 to present; active in Society of California Archivists, 1974 to present; active in Society of American Archivists, 1977 to present. Publications: *Clown Princes and Court Jesters*, with Kalton C. Lahue, 1970; *Day the Laughter Stopped*, 1976; *Paramount Collection Inventory*, 1977. Academy of Motion Picture Arts and Sciences, 8949 Wilshire Boulevard, Beverly Hills, CA 90211.

GITT, ROBERT R., film archivist. b. December 6, 1941, Hanover, Pennsylvania; B.A., Dartmouth College, 1963; technical officer, American Film Institute, 1970–1975; preservation supervisor, UCLA Film Archives, 1977 to present; responsible for many major film restorations, including *Becky Sharp*, *Bullfighter and the Lady*, *Lost Horizon*, Orson Welles's *Macbeth*, and *The Toll of the Sea*. 4118 Rhodes Avenue, Studio City, CA 91604.

GLOVER, WILLIAM, theatre critic. b. May 6, 1911, New York; Litt.B., Rutgers University, 1932; theatre writer, Associated Press, 1953 to present; theatre critic, Associated Press, 1960–1978. 4 East 88 Street, New York, NY 10128.

GOMERY, DOUGLAS, professor of film and television. b. April 5, 1945, New York; B.S., Lehigh University, 1967; M.A., University of Wisconsin, Madison, 1970; Ph.D., University of Wisconsin, Madison, 1975; associate professor, Department of Communication Arts and Theatre, University of Maryland, 1981 to present; member, Board of Trustees, American Film Institute, 1986 to present. Publications: *Film History: Theory and Practice*, with Robert C. Allen, 1985; *The Hollywood Studio System*, 1986. 4817 Drummond Avenue, Chevy Chase, MD 20815.

GREEN, STANLEY, theatre historian. b. May 29, 1923, New York; B.A., Union College, Schenectady, 1943. Publications: *The World of Musical Comedy*, 1960, 1980; *The Rodgers and Hammerstein Story* 1963; *Ring Bells! Sing Songs!*, 1971; *Starring Fred Astaire*, 1973; *Encyclopaedia of the Musical Theatre*, 1976, 1980; *Broadway Musicals*, 1977; *Rodgers and Hammerstein*, 1980; *Encyclopaedia of Musical Film*, 1981; *The Great Clowns of Broadway*, 1984. 169 State Street, Brooklyn, NY 11201.

GREENSPUN, ROGER, film critic. b. December 16, 1929, Bridgeport, Connecticut; B.A., Yale University, 1951; M.A., Yale University, 1958; film critic, *The New York Times*, 1969–1973; film critic, *Penthouse*, 1973 to present. Penthouse, 909 Third Avenue, New York, NY 10022.

GRESSLEY, GENE M., archivist. b. June 20, 1931, Frankfort, Indiana; B.S., Manchester University, 1952; M.A., Indiana University, 1956; Ph.D., University of Oregon, 1964; director, school of American studies, University of Wyoming, 1969–1976; assistant to the president, American Heritage Center, University of Wyoming, 1976–1986; assistant to the president, American Heritage Center, and assistant to the vice-president for development, University of Wyoming, 1986 to present. Publications: *Bankers and Cattlemen,* 1966; *The American West: A Reorientation,* 1967; *West by East: The American West in the Gilded Age,* 1972; *Bostonians and Bullion,* 1975; *The Great Plains Experience,* 1975; *Advocates and Adversaries: The Life and Times of Robert R. Rose,* 1977; *The Twentieth-Century West: A Potpourri,* 1977; *Voltaire and the Cowboy: The Letters of Thurman Arnold,* 1977. University of Wyoming, Laramie, WY 82071.

GUERNSEY, OTIS L., JR., drama critic and editor. b. August 9, 1918, New York; B.A., Yale University, 1940; staff member, *New York Herald Tribune,* 1941–1960; editor, *The Best Plays* series, 1963–1966; editor, *Dramatists Guild Quarterly,* 1964 to present; editor, *The Burns Mantle Yearbook of the Theatre* series, 1965–1978. Publications: *Diary of the American Theatre, 1964–1971,* 1971; *Playwrights, Lyricists, and Composers on Theatre,* 1974. North Pomfret, VT 05053.

GUILES, FRED LAWRENCE, writer. b. November 17, 1920, Des Moines, Iowa; B.S., Columbia University, 1950; Publications: *Norma Jean: The Life of Marilyn Monroe,* 1969; *Marion Davies,* 1973; *Hanging on in Paradise,* 1975; *Tyrone Power: The Last Idol,* 1979; *Stan: The Life of Stan Laurel,* 1981; *Jane Fonda: The Actress in Her Time,* 1982. c/o Franklin R. Weissberg, 505 Park Avenue, New York, NY 10022.

GUSSOW, MEL, theatre critic. b. December 19, 1933, New York; B.A., Middlebury College, 1955; M.S., Columbia University, 1956; drama critic, *The New York Times,* 1969 to present. Publications: *Don't Say Yes until I Finish Talking,* 1971, 1980. The New York Times, 229 West 43 Street, New York, NY 10036.

HANSON, PATRICIA KING, film writer and editor. b. January 9, 1947, Los Angeles; B.A., University of Southern California, 1968; M.A., University of Southern California, 1970; M.L.S., University of Southern California, 1974; history bibliographer, University of Southern California, 1972–1978; associate editor, Salem Press, 1978–1983; executive editor, American Film Institute Catalog of Feature Films, 1911–1920 and 1931–1940, 1983 to present; film critic, *Screen International,* 1987 to present. Publications: *Magill's Bibliography of Literary Criticism,* co-associate editor, 1979; *Magill's Survey of Cinema, English Language Films, Series I,* co-associate editor, 1980; *Magill's Survey of Cinema, English Language Films, Series II*, co-associate editor, 1981; *Magill's Survey of Cinema, Silent Films*, co-associate editor, 1982; *Magill's Cinema Annual 1982*, co-associate editor, 1983; *Magill's Cinema Annual 1983*, associate editor, 1984; *Magill's Survey of Cinema, Foreign Language Films*, co-associate editor, 1985; *Film Review Index, Vol. I, 1882–1949*, co-editor, 1986; *Film Review Index, Vol. II, 1950–1985*, co-editor, 1987. 133½ North Hamilton Drive, Beverly Hills, CA 90211.

HANSON, STEPHEN L., film librarian and writer. b. September 20, 1942, Los Angeles; B.A., Long Beach State College, 1967; M.S.L.S., University of Southern California, 1969; M.A., University of Southern California, 1973; performing arts bibliographer, University of Southern California, 1969 to present; film critic, *Screen International*, 1987 to present; editor, *Coronto*. Publications: *Magill's Bibliography of Literary Criticism*, co-associate editor, 1979; *Magill's Survey of Cinema, English Language Films, Series I*, co-associate editor, 1980; *Magill's Survey of Cinema, English Language Films, Series II*, co-associate editor, 1981; *Magill's Survey of Cinema, Silent Films*, co-associate editor, 1982; *Magill's Cinema Annual, 1982*, co-associate editor, 1983; *Film Review Index, Vol. I, 1882–1949*, co-editor, 1986; *Film Review Index, Vol. II, 1950–1985*, co-editor, 1987. 133½ North Hamilton Drive, Beverly Hills, CA 90211.

HARBIN, VERNON S., film consultant and archivist. b. January 17, 1909, Petrolia, Texas; RKO Pictures staff member, 1931 to present; currently consultant and archivist emeritus for RKO Pictures, Inc. Publication: *The RKO Story*, with Richard B. Jewell, 1982. 386 S. Burnside Avenue, Apt. 1-H, Los Angeles, CA 90036.

HART, HENRY, film critic and editor. b. September 14, 1903, Philadelphia; editor, *Films in Review*, 1950–1972. Publications: *The Great One*, 1934; *The American Writers Congress*, editor, 1935; *The Writer in a Changing World*, editor, 1937. 308 Pennsylvania Avenue, Spring Lake, NJ 07762.

HASKELL, MOLLY, writer and critic. Former critic, *The Village Voice, Viva, New York*, and *All Things Considered* (National Public Radio); film reviewer, *Vogue*. Publication: *From Reverence to Rape: The Treatment of Women in the Movies*, 1973. 19 East 88 Street, New York, NY 10128.

HIGHAM, CHARLES, writer, poet, and biographer. b. February 18, 1931, London; literary editor, *Bulletin* (Sydney, Australia), 1963–1968; regents professor, University of California at Santa Cruz, 1969. Selected Publications: *Hollywood in the Forties*, with Joel Greenberg, 1968; *The Films of Orson Welles*, 1970; *The Art of the American Film*, 1973; *Kate: The Life of Katharine Hepburn*, 1975; *Marlene: The Life of Marlene Dietrich*, 1977; *Errol*

Flynn: The Untold Story, 1980; *Bette: The Life of Bette Davis*, 1981; *Audrey: The Life of Audrey Hepburn*, 1984; *Orson Welles: The Rise and Fall of an American Genius*, 1985; *Lucy: The Life of Lucille Ball*, 1986. 4027 Farmouth Drive, Los Angeles, CA 90027.

HITCHENS, GORDON, professor of film, journalist, festival consultant. b. March 3, 1925, California; B.S., Columbia University, 1960; M.A., Columbia University, 1961; M.F.A., Columbia University, 1962; founder and editor of *Film Comment*, 1962–1970; professor of film, C. W. Post University; agent for Nyon International Film Festival, International Filmfestspiele Berlin and Hemisfilm International Film Festival. 214 West 85 Street, Apt. 3W, New York, NY 10024.

HOFFER, THOMAS WILLIAM, mass communication professor. b. May 31, 1938, Toledo, Ohio; B.A., University of Iowa, 1960; M.A., University of Wisconsin at Madison, 1969; Ph.D., University of Wisconsin at Madison, 1972; professor of mass communication, Florida State University, 1972 to present. Publication: *Animation: A Reference Guide*, 1981. 1810 Mayfair Drive, Tallahassee, FL 32303.

HORAK, JAN-CHRISTOPHER, film curator and critic. b. May 1, 1951, Bad Muenstereifel, Germany; B.A., University of Delaware, 1973; M.Sc., Boston University, 1975; Ph.D., Westfaelische Wilhelms-Universitaet, Munich, 1984; associate curator, film department, international museum of photography at George Eastman House, 1984 to present; part-time assistant professor, University of Rochester, 1984 to present. Publications: *Middle European Émigrés in Hollywood (1933–1945)*, 1977; *Film und Foto der zwanziger Jahre*, co-editor, 1979; *Helmar Lerski—Lichtbildner*, with Ute Eskildsen, 1982; *Fluchtpunkt Hollywood: Eine Dokumentation zur Filmemigration nach 1933*, 1984, 1986; *Anti-Nazi-Filme der deutschsprachigen Emigration von Hollywood 1939–1946*, 1984, 1986. 502 Cedarwood Terrace, Rochester, NY 14609.

HORTON, ANDREW S., professor of film and literature. b. October 10, 1944, Charlottesville, Virginia; B.A., Hamilton College, 1966; M.A., Colgate University, 1969; Ph.D., University of Illinois, 1973; professor of film and literature, English department, University of New Orleans, 1977 to present; also screenwriter. Publications: *Selected Short Plays of Costas Marsellas*, 1975; *Modern European Filmmakers and the Art of Adaptation*, 1981; *The Films of George Roy Hill*, 1984. 814 Independence Street, New Orleans, LA 70117.

HOUSTON, BEVERLE A., professor of film. b. December 23, 1935, Reading, Pennsylvania; B.A., University of Pennsylvania, 1957; M.A., University of Pennsylvania, 1961; Ph.D., University of California at Los Angeles, 1969; professor of English and film, Pitzer College, 1970–1982;

professor of film studies and director of critical studies division, school of cinema-television, University of Southern California, 1982 to present. Publications: *Close-Up: A Critical Perspective on Film*, with Marsha Kinder, 1972; *Self and Cinema: A Transformationalist Perspective*, with Marsha Kinder, 1980. 840 N. Occidental Boulevard, Los Angeles, CA 90026.

HUMPHRYS, BARBARA, librarian. b. April 21, 1943, San Diego; B.A., University of Wyoming, 1965; M.S.L.S., University of Illinois, 1967; librarian, Motion Picture, Broadcasting, and Recorded Sound Division, Library of Congress. Motion Picture, Broadcasting, and Recorded Sound Division, Library of Congress, Washington, DC 20540.

JACOBS, DIANE, film critic and writer. b. October 26, 1948, New York; B.A., University of Pennsylvania, 1970; M.F.A., Columbia University, 1973; professional writer, contributing to *Soho Weekly News*, *Paperback News*, *Horizon*, and others. Publications: *Hollywood Renaissance*, 1977; *But We Need the Eggs: The Magic of Woody Allen*, 1982. 220 East 63 Street, New York, NY 10021.

JACOBS, LEWIS, film scholar. b. April 22, 1906, Philadelphia; trained as a painter; producer, director and writer in Hollywood, 1940–1950; staff director and writer for MPO Productions and free-lance documentary producer-director; recipient of Silver Star Award from Philadelphia College of Art, 1976; recipient of award from National Endowment for the Arts to research companion volume to *The Rise of the American Film*, 1981. Publications: *The Rise of the American Film*, 1939; *Introduction to the Art of the Movies*, 1960; *The Emergence of Film Art*, 1969; *The Movies as Medium*, 1970; *The Documentary Tradition*, 1971; *The International Encyclopedia of Film*, American Advisory Editor, 1972; *The Compound Cinema*, 1977. 9 Grace Court West, Great Neck, NY 11021.

JEWELL, RICHARD B., professor of film. b. November 14, 1945, Nashville, Tennessee; B.A., Vanderbilt University, 1967; M.A., University of Florida, 1968; Ph.D., University of Southern California, 1978; professor of film, University of Southern California, school of cinema-television, 1976 to present. Publications: *Primary Cinema Resources*, with Christopher Wheaton, 1975; *The RKO Story*, 1982. School of Cinema-Television, University of Southern California, Los Angeles, CA 90089–2211.

JOWETT, GARTH S., professor of communication. b. March 2, 1940, Cape Town, South Africa; B.A., York University, 1968; M.A., University of Pennsylvania, 1971; Ph.D., University of Pennsylvania, 1972; assistant professor, Carleton University, 1971–1974; associate professor, University of Windsor, 1974–1976; head and professor, department of communication studies, University of Windsor, 1976–1979; director and professor, school of communication, University of Houston, 1980–1985; professor, school of communication, University of Houston, 1985 to present. Publications: *Film: The Democratic Art*, 1976; *Movies as Mass Communication*, with James M. Linton, 1980; *Propaganda and Persuasion*, with Victoria O'Donnell, 1986. 4371 Varsity Lane, Houston, TX 77004.

KAEL, PAULINE, film critic. b. June 19, 1919, Sonoma County, California; Guggenheim Fellow, 1964; George Polk Memorial Award for Criticism, 1970; many honorary degrees; movie critic at *The New Yorker*, 1968 to present. Publications: *I Lost It at the Movies*, 1965; *Kiss Kiss Bang Bang*, 1968; *Going Steady*, 1970; *The Citizen Kane Book*, 1971; *Deeper into Movies*, 1973; *Reeling*, 1976; *When the Lights Go Down*, 1980; *5001 Nights at the Movies*, 1982; *Taking It All In*, 1984; *State of the Art*, 1985. c/o The New Yorker, 25 West 43 Street, New York, NY 10036.

KAMINSKY, STUART M., professor of film. b. September 29, 1934, Chicago, Illinois; B.S., University of Illinois, 1957; M.A., University of Illinois, 1960; Ph.D., Northwestern University, 1971; professor of radio, television, and film, head of program in creative writing for the media, Northwestern University. Publications: *Don Siegel: Director*, 1973; *Clint Eastwood*, 1974; *American Film Genres: Approaches to a Critical Theory of Popular Film*, 1974, 1977, 1984; *Ingmar Bergman: Essays in Criticism*, 1975; *John Huston: Maker of Magic*, 1978; *Bullet for a Star*, 1978; *Murder on the Yellow Brick Road*, 1979; *You Bet Your Life*, 1980; *The Howard Hughes Affair*, 1980; *Never Cross a Vampire*, 1980, 1984; *Coop: The Life and Legend of Gary Cooper*, 1980; *Basic Filmmaking*, with Dana Hodgdon, 1981; *Death of a Dissident*, 1981; *High Midnight*, 1981, 1984; *Catch a Falling Clown*, 1982, 1984; *He Done Her Wrong*, 1983; *When the Dark Man Calls*, 1983; *Black Knight on Red Square*, 1983; *American Television Genres*, with Jeffrey Mahan, 1984; *Down for the Count*, 1985; *Red Chameleon*, 1985; *Exercise in Terror*, 1985. 1725 Monroe, Evanston, IL 60202.

KAPLAN, E. ANN, professor of English and film. b. December 8, 1936, Newcastle, United Kingdom; B.A., University of Birmingham, England, 1958; Postgraduate Diploma in English, London University, 1959; Ph.D., Rutgers University, 1970; associate professor in English, Rutgers University, 1979–1987; director, the humanities institute, State University of New York at Stony Brook, 1987 to present. Publications: *Talking about the Cinema*, with Jim Kitses, 1963, 1974; *Women in Film Noir: An Anthology*, 1978; *Fritz Lang: A Guide to References and Resources*, 1981; *Re-Garding Television: A Critical Anthology*, 1983; *Women and Film: Both Sides of the Camera*, 1983; *Rocking around the Clock: Music Television, Postmodernism and Consumer Cul-*

ture, 1987; *Motherhood and Representation*, 1987. The Humanities Institute, State University of New York, Stony Brook, NY 11794–3391.

KAUFFMANN, STANLEY, film and theatre critic. b. April 24, 1916, New York; B.F.A., New York University, 1935; film critic, *The New Republic*; visiting professor, theater department, graduate center of the City University of New York. Publications: *A World on Film*, 1966, 1975; *Figures of Light*, 1971; *Persons of the Drama*, 1976; *Living Images*, 1978; *Before My Eyes*, 1980; *Theatre Criticisms*, 1983; *Field of View*, 1986. 10 West 15 Street, New York, NY 10011.

KAWIN, BRUCE, professor of English and film. b. November 6, 1945, Los Angeles; A.B., Columbia University, 1967; M.A., Cornell University, 1969; Ph.D., Cornell University, 1970; professor of English and film, University of Colorado, 1975 to present. Publications: *Telling It Again and Again: Repetition in Literature and Film*, 1972; *Faulkner and Film*, 1977; *Mindscreen: Bergman, Godard, and First-Person Film*, 1978; *To Have and Have Not*, editor, 1980; *The Mind of the Novel: Reflexive Fiction and the Ineffable*, 1982; *Faulkner's MGM Screenplays*, 1982; *How Movies Work*, 1986. 915 15th Street, Boulder, CO 80302.

KERR, WALTER, drama critic. b. July 8, 1913, Evanston, Illinois; B.S., Northwestern University, 1937; M.A., Northwestern University, 1938; drama critic, *Commonweal*, 1950–1952; drama critic, *New York Herald Tribune*, 1951–1966; drama critic, *The New York Times*, 1966 to present. Publications: *Criticism and Censorship*, 1954; *How Not To Write a Play*, 1955; *Pieces of Eight*, 1957; *The Decline of Pleasure*, 1962; *The Theatre in Spite of Itself*, 1963; *Tragedy and Comedy*, 1967; *Thirty Plays Hath September*, 1969; *God on the Gymnasium Floor*, 1971; *The Silent Clowns*, 1975; *Journey to the Center of the Theater*, 1979. 1 Beach Avenue, Larchmont, NY 10538.

KINDER, MARSHA, professor of film. b. February 20, 1940, Los Angeles; A.B., University of California at Los Angeles, 1961; M.A., University of California at Los Angeles, 1963; Ph.D., University of California at Los Angeles, 1966; professor of critical studies in cinema-television, University of Southern California, 1980 to present. Publications: *Close-Up: A Critical Perspective on Film*, with Beverle A. Houston, 1972; *Self and Cinema: A Transformationalist Perspective*, with Beverle A. Houston, 1980. 2021 Holly Hill Terrace, Los Angeles, CA 90068.

KNIGHT, ARTHUR, film critic and professor of film. b. September 3, 1916, Philadelphia, Pennsylvania; B.A., CCNY, 1940; film critic, *Saturday Review*, 1949–1973; film critic, *The Hollywood Reporter*; professor of film, University of Southern California, 1960–1986. Publications: *The Liveliest*

Art, 1957, 1978; *The Hollywood Style*, 1969; *Playboy's Sex in the Cinema*, with Hollis Alpert, 1971; *Playboy's Sex in the Cinema 2*, with Hollis Alpert, 1972; *Playboy's Sex in the Cinema 3*, with Hollis Alpert, 1973; *Playboy's Sex in the Cinema 4*, 1974; *Playboy's Sex in the Cinema 5*, 1975; *Playboy's Sex in the Cinema 6*, 1976. 22202 Pacific Coast Highway, Malibu, CA 90265.

KNUTSON, ROBERT L., librarian. B.S., University of Southern California; M.A., University of California at Berkeley; Ph.D., Columbia University; M.S.L.S., University of Southern California; head, department of special collections, University of Southern California Library, 1963–1985; head, cinema/TV library, University of Southern California, 1985–1987. 2127 Stanley Hills Drive, Los Angeles, CA 90046.

KOSZARSKI, RICHARD, film historian. b. December 18, 1947, New York; B.A., Hofstra University, 1969; M.A., New York University, 1974; Ph.D., New York University, 1977; associate professor of film, Columbia University; editor, *Film History, an International Journal*; curator of film, American Museum of the Moving Image; historical consultant and narration scriptwriter on 1978 film project, *Roger Corman, Hollywood's Wild Angel*; writer, researcher and co-director on 1979 film project, *The Man You Loved To Hate*. Publications: *The Rivals of D. W. Griffith*, 1976; *Hollywood Directors, 1914–1940*, 1976; *Hollywood Directors, 1941–1976*, 1977; *Universal Pictures: 65 Years*, 1977; *Mystery of the Wax Museum*, editor, 1979; *The Astoria Studio and Its Fabulous Films*, 1983; *The Man You Loved To Hate*, 1983; *History of the American Film, 1915–1927*, 1987. American Museum of the Moving Image, 34–12 36th Street, Astoria, NY 11106.

KOWALL, LINDA, journalist. b. July 2, 1950, Abington, Pennsylvania; B.A., Beaver College; curator, "Peddler of Dreams, Siegmund Lubin and the Creation of the Motion Picture Industry," with Joseph Eckhardt, museum exhibit and catalog, National Museum of American Jewish History, 1984. 60 Bayberry Road, Huntingdon Valley, PA 19006.

KRAFSUR, RICHARD, magazine editor and publisher. b. December 16, 1940, New York; B.A., George Washington University, 1965; M.Phil., George Washington University, 1970; editor and publisher, *Emmy* magazine, 1981–1986; consulting editor and publisher, *Television & Families*. Publication: *American Film Institute Catalog: Feature Films 1961–1970*, editor, 1976. 3457 Adina Drive, Los Angeles, CA 90068.

KRAMER, EDITH, film curator. b. April 7, 1934, New York; M.A., Harvard University, Radcliffe College; film curator and director, Pacific Film Archives. 2625 Durant Avenue, Berkeley, CA 94720.

KREUGER, MILES, theatre and film historian. b. March 28, 1934, New York; B.A., Bard College; president and founder of The Institute of the American Musical, Inc. Publications: *The Movie Musical from Vitaphone to 42nd Street,* 1975; *Souvenir Programs of Twelve Classic Movies: 1927–1941,* 1977; *Show Boat: The Story of a Classic American Musical,* 1977. 121 North Detroit Street, Los Angeles, CA 90036.

KUIPER, JOHN B., film archivist. b. June 22, 1928, Ann Arbor, Michigan; B.A., University of Kentucky; M.A., University of Iowa; Ph.D., University of Iowa; head, motion picture section and assistant chief for motion pictures, Library of Congress, 1965–1975; chief, prints and photographs division, Library of Congress, 1976–1977; director, department of film, International Museum of Photography at George Eastman House, 1977–1981; acting director, International Museum of Photography at George Eastman House, 1980–1981; director, film collections, International Museum of Photography at George Eastman House, 1981–1987; professor, department of English, University of Rochester, 1977–1987; chairperson, division of radio/TV/film, North Texas State University, 1987 to present. Publication: *A Handbook for Film Archives,* with Eileen Bowser, 1980. Division of Radio/TV/Film, North Texas State University, P.O. Box 13108, Denton, TX 76203–3108.

LAFFERTY, WILLIAM, professor of theatre arts. b. January 13, 1949, Oak Park, Illinois; B.S., Purdue University, 1972; M.A., Purdue University, 1977; Ph.D., Northwestern University, 1981; assistant professor, department of theatre arts, Wright State University, 1981–1986; associate professor of theatre arts, Wright State University, 1986 to present. Department of Theatre Arts, Wright State University, Dayton, OH 45435.

LAHR, JOHN, writer and theatre critic. b. July 12, 1941, Los Angeles; B.A., Yale University, 1963; M.A., Worcester College, Oxford, 1965; theatre critic, *The Nation,* 1981 to present; contributing editor, *Harper's,* 1979 to present. Selected Publications: *Notes on a Cowardly Lion: The Biography of Bert Lahr,* 1969; *Prick Up Your Ears: The Biography of Joe Orton,* 1978. c/o Alfred A. Knopf, 201 East 50 Street, New York, NY 10022.

LAHUE, KALTON C., writer. b. October 4, 1934, Richford, Vermont; B.S., University of Vermont, 1959; M.A., San Jose State College, 1967; author of more than twenty photography-related publications. Selected Publications: *Continued Next Week,* 1964; *The World of Laughter,* 1966; *Kops and Custards,* 1968; *Collecting Classic Films,* 1970; *Winners of the West,* 1970; *Dreams for Sale,* 1971; *Motion Picture Pioneer,* 1973. 1800 State Street, No. 46, Pasadena, CA 91030.

LEAB, DANIEL J., historian. b. August 29, 1936, Germany; B.A., Columbia College, 1957; M.A., Columbia University, 1961; Ph.D., Columbia University, 1969; faculty member, department of history, Seton Hall University, 1974 to present. Publications: *A Union of Individuals: The Origins of the American Newspaper Guild*, 1970; *From Sambo to Superspade: The Black Image on Film*, 1975; *The Auction Companion*, with Katharine Kyes Leab, 1980; *A Bibliography of American Working Class History*, with Dorothy Swanson and Maurice Neufeld, 1984. P.O. Box 216, Washington, CT 06793.

LENNIG, ARTHUR, professor of film. b. February 22, 1933, East Williston, New York; B.A., State University of New York, 1955; M.A., State University of New York, 1956; Ph.D., University of Wisconsin, 1961; associate professor of art in cinema, State University of New York at Albany. Publications: *Film Notes*, editor, 1960; *Classics of the Film*, editor, 1965; *The Silent Voice*, 1966, 1969; *The Sound Film*, 1969; *The Count: The Life and Films of Bela "Dracula" Lugosi*, 1974. 222 Third Street, Troy, NY 12180.

LENTHALL, FRANKLYN, theatre historian and curator. b. July 14, 1919, Nantiocke, Pennsylvania; founder and curator, Boothbay Theatre Museum, 1957 to present; also theatrical producer and director. Boothbay Theatre Museum, Corey Lane, Boothbay, ME 04537.

LEONARD, WILLIAM TORBERT, writer. b. October 26, 1918, Delaware. Publications: *Film Directors Guide: The United States*, with James Robert Parish, 1974; *Hollywood Players: The Forties*, with James Robert Parish, 1976; *Hollywood Players: The Thirties*, with James Robert Parish, 1976; *The Funsters*, with James Robert Parish, 1979; *Theatre: Stage to Screen to Television*, 1981; *Masquerade in Black*, 1987; *Once Was Enough*, 1987. 218 Biddulph Road, Radnor, PA 19087.

LEYDA, JAY, film scholar and professor. b. February 12, 1910, Detroit; faculty member, New York University. Publications: *An Index to the Creative Work of Alexander Dovzhenko*, 1947; *An Index to the Creative Work of Vsevelod Pudovkin*, 1948; *Kino*, 1960; *Films Beget Films*, 1964; *Dianying*, 1972; *Voices of Film Experience*, 1977; *Eisenstein at Work*, with Zina Voynow, 1982. 2 Washington Square Village, Apartment 12-H, New York, NY 10012.

LIMBACHER, JAMES, film historian and writer. b. November 30, 1926, St. Marys, Ohio; B.A., Bowling Green State University, 1949; M.A., Bowling Green State University, 1954; M.S.Ed., Indiana University, 1955; M.S.L.S., Wayne State University. Publications: *A Historical Study of the Color Motion Picture*, 1952; *Four Aspects of the Film*, 1969; *A Reference Guide to Audiovisual Information*, 1972; *Film Music: From Violins to Video*, 1974; *Haven't I Seen You Somewhere Before?*, 1979; *Keeping Score: Film Music 1972–*

118

SOURCEBOOK FOR THE PERFORMING ARTS

1979, 1981; *Sexuality in World Cinema,* 1983; *Feature Films,* 1985 (8th edition). 21800 Morley Avenue, Apt. 1201, Dearborn, MI 48124.

LONEY, GLENN MEREDITH, drama educator. b. December 24, 1928, Sacramento, California; A.B., University of California at Berkeley, 1950; M.A., University of Wisconsin, 1951; Ph.D., Stanford University, 1953; member of faculty, Brooklyn College and City University Graduate Center, 1961 to present; editor, *Art Deco News.* Publications: *Briefing and Conference Techniques,* 1959; *Peter Brook's A Midsummer Night's Dream,* 1974; *The Shakespeare Complex,* 1974; *Young Vic Scapino,* 1980; *Your Future in the Performing Arts,* 1980; *The House of Mirth: The Play of the Novel,* 1981; *California Gold Rush Drama,* 1984; *Musical Theatre in America,* 1984; *Unsung Genius,* 1984; *Staging Shakespeare,* 1986. 3 East 71 Street, New York, NY 10021.

LYONS, TIMOTHY J., professor of film. b. July 6, 1944, Framingham, Massachusetts; B.A., University of California at Santa Barbara, 1966; M.A., University of California at Santa Barbara, 1968; Ph.D., University of Iowa, 1972; professor and chairperson, Southern Illinois University at Carbondale, department of cinema and photography, 1980–1985; dean, college of fine and performing arts, Youngstown State University, 1985 to present. Publications: *The Silent Partner: The History of the American Film Manufacturing Company, 1910–1922,* 1974; *Glossary of Film Terms,* editor, 1978, 1979; *Charles Chaplin: A Guide to References and Resources,* 1979; *The Influence of the World Film Heritage on the Training and Education of Film/TV Directors and Communicators,* editor with Donald E. Staples and Robert W. Wagner, 1979; *The Core American Films,* editor, 1981. 658 Notre Dame Avenue, Austintown, OH 44515.

MacCANN, RICHARD DYER, professor of film. b. August 20, 1920, Wichita, Kansas; A.B., University of Kansas, 1940; M.A., Stanford University, 1942; Ph.D., Harvard University, 1951; staff correspondent, *The Christian Science Monitor,* 1951–1957; assistant professor of cinema, University of Southern California, 1957–1962; associate professor of speech and journalism, University of Kansas, 1965–1969; member of faculty, communication and theater arts department, University of Iowa, 1970 to present; editor, *Cinema Journal,* 1967–1976. Publications: *Hollywood in Transition,* 1962; *Film and Society,* 1964; *Film: A Montage of Theories,* 1966; *The People's Films,* 1973; *The New Film Index,* 1975; *Cinema Examined,* 1982. 717 Normandy Drive, Iowa City, IA 52240.

MALTIN, LEONARD, film critic and historian. b. December 18, 1950, New York; B.A., New York University; editor and publisher *Film Fan Monthly,* 1966–1975; film critic *Entertainment Tonight* and *Entertainment This Week;* contributor of weekly column of Movies on TV to *The New York*

Post. Publications: *Movie Comedy Teams,* 1970; *Behind the Camera: The Art of the Cinematographer,* 1971; *The Great Movie Shorts,* 1972; *The Disney Films,* 1973; *The Laurel and Hardy Book,* 1973; *Carole Lombard,* 1976; *Our Gang,* with Richard W. Bann, 1977; *The Great Movie Comedians from Charlie Chaplin to Woody Allen,* 1978; *Hollywood Kids,* 1978; *The Real Stars,* 1979; *Of Mice and Magic,* 1980; *The Whole Film Sourcebook,* 1983; *Leonard Maltin's TV Movies,* 1984. c/o Entertainment Tonight, 5555 Melrose Avenue, Hollywood, CA 90038.

MANCHEL, FRANK, professor of English and critic. b. July 22, 1935, Detroit, Michigan; A.B., Ohio State University, 1957; M.A., Hunter College, 1960; Ed.D., Teachers College, Columbia University, 1966; associate dean, college of arts and sciences, University of Vermont, 1977 to present; member of editorial board, *Journal of Popular Film and Television,* 1977 to present. Publications: *Movies and How They Are Made,* 1968; *When Pictures Began to Move,* 1968; *When Movies Began To Speak,* 1969; *Terrors of the Screen,* 1970; *Cameras West,* 1971; *Yesterday's Clowns: The Rise of Film Comedy,* 1973; *Film Study: A Resource Guide,* 1973; *The Talking Clowns,* 1976; *An Album of Great Science Fiction Films,* 1976, 1982; *Women on the Hollywood Screen,* 1977; *Gangsters on the Screen,* 1978; *The Box Office Clowns: From Bob Hope to Woody Allen,* 1979; *Great Sports Movies,* 1980; *An Album of Modern Horror Films,* 1983. R.R.1, Box No. 1373, Shelburne, VT 05482.

MARILL, ALVIN H., television historian. b. January 10, 1934, Brockton, Massachusetts; B.A., Boston University, 1955; executive editor, press information CBS Entertainment, 1984 to present. Publications: *The Cinema of Edward G. Robinson,* 1972; *The Films of Anthony Quinn,* 1975; *Samuel Goldwyn Presents,* 1976; *The Films of Sidney Poitier,* 1976; *Moe Howard and the 3 Stooges,* editor, 1977; *Robert Mitchum on the Screen,* 1977; *The Films of Tyrone Power,* 1979; *Movies Made for Television, 1964–1979,* 1980; *Movies Made for Television, 1964–1984,* 1984; *Movies Made for Television, 1964–1986,* 1987. 511 Doremus Avenue, Glen Rock, NJ 07452.

MAST, GERALD, professor of film. b. May 13, 1940, Los Angeles; B.A., University of Chicago, 1961; M.A., University of Chicago, 1962; Ph.D., University of Chicago, 1967; program coordinator and developer of curriculum, Cinema Studies Department, Richmond College, CUNY, 1969–1978; developer of film studies curriculum and film archive and study center, University of Chicago, 1978 to present. Publications: *A Short History of the Movies,* 1971; *The Comic Mind: Comedy and the Movies,* 1973; *Filmguide to "Rules of the Game,"* 1973; *Film Theory and Criticism: Introductory Readings,* with Marshall Cohen, 1974; *Film/Cinema/Movie: A Theory of Experience,* 1977; *The Movies in Our Midst: Readings in the Cultural History of Film in America,* 1982; *Howard Hawks: Storyteller,* 1982; *Can't Help Singin': The*

American Musical on Stage and Screen, 1986. 5442 Ridgewood Court, Chicago, IL 60615.

McBRIDE, JOSEPH, film critic and writer. b. August 9, 1947, Milwaukee, Wisconsin; reporter and critic, *Daily Variety*, 1974–1977; writer for AFI Life Achievement Award salutes to James Stewart, Fred Astaire, Frank Capra, John Huston, and Lillian Gish; also screenwriter. Publications: *Persistence of Vision*, editor, 1968; *Orson Welles*, 1972; *Focus on Howard Hawks*, editor, 1972; *John Ford*, with Michael Wilmington, 1974, 1975; *Kirk Douglas*, 1976; *Orson Welles: Actor and Director*, 1977; *Hawks on Hawks*, 1982; *Filmmakers on Filmmaking*, editor, 1983. c/o Writers Guild/West, 8955 Beverly Boulevard, Los Angeles, CA 90048.

McCABE, JOHN C., professor of drama and writer. b. November 14, 1920, Detroit, Michigan; Ph.B., University of Detroit, 1947; M.F.A., Fordham University, 1948; Ph.D., The Shakespeare Institute, 1954; formerly chairman, department of dramatic art, New York University; retired. Publications: *Mr. Laurel and Mr. Hardy*, 1961; *George M. Cohan: The Man Who Owned Broadway*, 1973; *The Comedy World of Stan Laurel*, 1975; *Laurel & Hardy*, with Al Kilgore and R. W. Bann, 1975; *Cagney by Cagney*, ghostwriter, 1976; *Proclaiming the Word*, with G. B. Harrison, 1977; *Charlie Chaplin*, 1978; *Grand Hotel: Mackinac Island*, 1987; *Babe: The Life of Oliver Hardy*, 1988. 967 74th Street, Brooklyn, NY 11228 (November–March), Box 363, Mackinac Island, MI 49757 (April–October).

McCARTHY, TODD, film reporter and critic. b. 1950, Evanston, Illinois; B.A., Stanford University, 1972; reporter and critic, *Variety* and *Daily Variety*, 1979 to present. Publication: *Kings of the Bs: Working within the Hollywood System*, 1975. *Daily Variety*, 1400 N. Cahuenga Boulevard, Los Angeles, CA 90028.

McCARTY, CLIFFORD, film scholar. b. June 13, 1929, Los Angeles; B.A., California State University, Los Angeles, 1952; vice-president and editor of publications, Society for the Preservation of Film Music. Publications: *Film Composers in America: A Checklist of Their Work*, 1953; *Bogey: The Films of Humphrey Bogart*, 1965; *The Films of Errol Flynn*, with Tony Thomas and Rudy Behlmer, 1969; *Published Screenplays: A Checklist*, 1971; *The Films of Frank Sinatra*, with Gene Ringgold, 1971. P.O. Box 89, Topanga, CA 90290.

McNAMARA, BROOKS, professor of performance studies. b. February 1, 1937, Peoria, Illinois; B.A., Knox College, 1959; M.A., University of Iowa, 1961; Ph.D., Tulane University, 1965; professor of performance studies, New York University, 1968 to present; director, Shubert Archive. Publications: *The*

American Playhouse in the Eighteenth Century, 1969; *Step Right Up*, 1976; *Theatre Spaces and Environments*, with Richard Schechner and Jerry Rojo, 1976; *The Drama Review: Thirty Years of Commentary on the Avant-Garde*, co-editor with Jill Dolan, 1986. Department of Performance Studies, New York University, 721 Broadway, 6th Floor, New York, NY 10003.

MEHR, LINDA HARRIS, library administrator and film historian. b. July 1, 1939, Los Angeles; B.A., University of California at Los Angeles, 1961; M.A., University of California at Los Angeles, 1964; Ph.D., University of California at Los Angeles, 1973; visiting lecturer in history/communications, University of California at San Diego, 1979–1982; archivist, urban archives center, California State University, Northridge, 1981–1982; library administrator, Margaret Herrick Library, Academy of Motion Picture Arts and Sciences, 1982 to present. Publication: *Motion Pictures, Television and Radio: A Union Catalogue of Manuscript and Special Collections in the Western United States*, 1977. Academy of Motion Picture Arts and Sciences, 8949 Wilshire Boulevard, Beverly Hills, CA 90211.

MELLEN, JOAN, professor of film. b. September 7, 1941, New York; B.A., Hunter College, 1962; M.A., Graduate School and University Center of the City University of New York, 1964; Ph.D., Graduate School and University Center of the City University of New York, 1968; associate professor, Temple University, 1973–1976; professor of English, Temple University, 1977 to present. Publications: *A Film Guide to the Battle of Algiers*, 1973; *Marilyn Monroe*, 1973; *Women and Their Sexuality in the New Film*, 1973; *Voices from the Japanese Cinema*, 1975; *The Waves at Genji's Door: Japan through Its Cinema*, 1976; *Big Bad Wolves: Masculinity in the American Film*, 1978; *The World of Luis Buñuel*, editor, 1979; *Natural Tendencies*, 1981. 25 Elm Ridge Road, Pennington, NJ 08534.

MICHAELS, LLOYD, professor of English. b. March 4, 1945, New York; B.A., Brandeis University, 1966; M.A., Ohio University, 1967; Ph.D., SUNY, Buffalo, 1972; chairman, English department, Allegheny College; editor, *Film Criticism*. Publication: *Elia Kazan: A Guide to References and Resources*, 1985. Box D, Allegheny College, Meadville, PA 16335.

MONACO, JAMES, writer and publisher. b. 1942, New York; A.B., Muhlenberg College, 1963; M.A., Columbia University, 1964; member of faculty, New York School for Social Research, 1967 to present; founder and president, New York Zoetrope, Inc., 1975 to present; founder and president, Baseline, Inc., 1982 to present. Publications: *The New Wave: Godard, Truffaut, Chabrol, Rohmer, Rivette*, 1976; *How To Read a Film*, 1977; *Celebrity: The Media as Image Makers*, 1978; *Media Culture*, 1978; *Alain Resnais: The Role of Imagination*, 1978; *American Film Now*, 1979; *Who's Who in*

American Film Now, 1981; *The Connoisseurs Guide to the Movies*, 1985. 80 East 11 Street, New York, NY 10003.

MOSS, CARLTON, professor of film and film producer. b. February 14, 1911, Newark, New Jersey; lecturer, program in comparative culture, school of social sciences, University of California at Irvine, 1968 to present. Publication: *In Person—Lena Horne*, with Helen Arstein, 1950. 8954 Hollywood Hills Road, Hollywood, CA 90046.

MUSSER, CHARLES, film scholar and film maker. b. January 16, 1953, Stamford, Connecticut; B.A., Yale University, 1975; M.A., New York University, 1979; Ph.D., New York University, 1986; producer, director and editor, documentary, *An American Potter*, 1976; film historian, Thomas A. Edison Papers, Rutgers University project, 1980 to present; producer, director, co-writer, and editor, documentary, *Before the Nickelodeon*, 1982; co-curator, film series, *Before Hollywood*, for American Federation of the Arts, 1983 to present. Box 820, Times Square Station, New York, NY 10108.

NAREMORE, JAMES O., professor of English. b. April 7, 1941, Shreveport, Louisiana; B.A., Louisiana State University, 1963; M.A., Louisiana State University, 1965; Ph.D., University of Wisconsin, 1969; assistant professor, Indiana University, 1969–1972; associate professor, Indiana University, 1973–1977; professor of English and comparative literature, Indiana University, 1977 to present; director of film studies, Indiana University, 1976–1977, 1979–1980, 1982–1983, 1987 to present. Publications: *The World Without Self*, 1973; *The Filmguide to Psycho.* 1973; *The Magic World of Orson Welles*, 1978. Department of English, Ballantine Hall, Indiana University, Bloomington, IN 47405.

NELSON, RICHARD ALAN, professor of communication. b. February 22, 1947, Chicago; A.B., Stanford University, 1969; M.A., Brigham Young University, 1975; Ph.D., Florida State University, 1980; associate professor of communication, University of Houston. Publications: *Florida and the American Motion Picture Industry, 1898–1980*, 1983; *Propaganda: A Reference Guide*, 1987. School of Communication, 621 AH, University of Houston, University Park, Houston, TX 77004.

NICHOLS, WILLIAM J., film professor. b. August 19, 1942, New York; B.A., Duke University; M.A., University of California at Los Angeles; Ph.D., University of California at Los Angeles; professor of film studies, Queen's University. Publications: *Movies and Methods*, 1976; *Ideology and the Image*, 1981. Film Studies Department, Queen's University, Kingston, Ontario K7L 3N6, Canada.

O'CONNOR, JOHN, professor of history. b. August 13, 1943, New York; B.A., St. John University, 1965; M.A., Queens College (CUNY), 1967; Ph.D., CUNY Graduate Center, 1974; professor of history, New Jersey Institute of Technology, 1969 to present; co-founder and co-editor, *Film & History*, 1971 to present. Publications: *Teaching History with Film*, with Martin A. Jackson, 1974; *Film and the Humanities*, editor, 1977; *William Paterson: Lawyer and Statesman, 1745–1806*, 1979; *American History/American Film: Interpreting the Hollywood Image*, with Martin A. Jackson, 1979; *The Hollywood Indian*, 1981; *I Am a Fugitive from a Chain Gang*, editor, 1981; *American History/American Television: Interpreting the Video Past*, editor, 1983; *Looking at New Jersey: Photography as Social History, 1850–1915*, co-author, 1987. Department of Humanities, New Jersey Institute of Technology, Newark, NJ 07102.

OLIVER, EDITH, theatre critic. b. August 11, 1913, New York; member of editorial staff, *The New Yorker*, 1947 to present; off-Broadway reviewer, *The New Yorker*, 1961 to present; dramaturge, Eugene O'Neill Theatre Center, 1971–1980. The New Yorker, 25 West 43 Street, New York, NY 10036.

PARISH, JAMES ROBERT, marketing executive, film historian, and biographer. b. April 21, 1946, Cambridge, Massachusetts; B.A., University of Pennsylvania; LL.B., University of Pennsylvania; former reporter for *Variety* and publicist; founder of Entertainment Copyright Research Co., Inc. and JRP Media, Inc. Selected Publications: *The Emmy Awards*, 1970; *The MGM Stock Company*, 1972; *Liza!*, 1975; *Hollywood on Hollywood*, 1978; *The Great American Movies Book*, 1980; *The Best of MGM*, 1983. 2255 Ben Lomond Drive, Los Angeles, CA 90027.

PARKER, DAVID LAMBERT, curator. b. June 12, 1935, Roanoke, Virginia; B.A., University of Charleston, 1957; M.A., Ohio State University, 1959; staff member, motion picture, broadcasting, and sound division, Library of Congress, 1969 to present. Publications: *A Filmography of Films about Movie-Making*, 1972; *The Contract Director*, co-author, 1976; *Guide to Dance in Film*, with Esther Siegel, 1978. 14 Guy Court, Rockville, MD 20850.

PAVETTI, SALLY THOMAS, curator. b. August 15, 1936, New York; B.A., Wellesley College, 1958; M.A., Yale University, 1959; curator, Eugene O'Neill Theater Center, 1966 to present. Monte Cristo Cottage, 325 Pequot Avenue, New London, CT 06320.

PEARY, GERALD, film critic. b. October 30, 1944; B.A., Rider College, 1964; M.A., New York University, 1966; Ph.D., University of Wisconsin at Madison, 1977; associate professor, journalism and film, Suffolk University, 1980 to present; contributing editor, *American Film*. Publications:

Rita Hayworth, 1977; *The Classic American Novel and the Movies*, editor with Roger Shatzkin, 1977; *Women and the Cinema*, editor with Karyn Kay, 1977; *The Modern American Novel and the Movies*, editor with Roger Shatzkin, 1978; *The American Animated Cartoon*, editor with Danny Peary, 1980; *Little Caesar*, editor, 1981. 139 Antrim Street, Cambridge, MA 02139.

PERRY, EDWARD S. (TED), professor of film. b. June 4, 1937, New Orleans, Louisiana; B.A., Baylor University, 1960; M.A., University of Iowa, 1966; Ph.D., University of Iowa, 1968; director, department of film, Museum of Modern Art, 1975–1978; dean of arts and humanities, dean for program development, professor of theatre arts, Middlebury College, 1978–1981; professor of theatre arts and art, Middlebury College, 1982 to present; visiting professor, American Film Institute, center for advanced film studies, 1984 to present; member, board of trustees, American Film Institute, 1980 to present; member, board of directors, Anthology Film Archives, 1983 to present. Publications: *Fellini's 8½*, 1974; *Performing Arts Resources*, editor, 1975–1976; *The Film Index*, with Richard Dyer MacCann, 1975. Wright Theatre, Middlebury College, Middlebury, VT 05753.

PHILLIPS, REV. GENE D., professor of English. b. March 3, 1935, Springfield, Ohio; B.A., Loyola University, Chicago; M.A., Loyola University, Chicago; Ph.D., Fordham University; professor of English, Loyola University, Chicago. Publications: *The Movie Makers: Artists in an Industry*, 1973; *Graham Greene: The Films of His Fiction*, 1974; *Stanley Kubrick, a Film Odyssey*, 1975; *Ken Russell*, 1979; *Hemingway and Film*, 1980; *The Films of Tennessee Williams*, 1980; *John Schlesinger*, 1981; *George Cukor*, 1982; *Alfred Hitchcock*, 1984; *Fiction, Film and F. Scott Fitzgerald*, 1986. Loyola University, Faculty Residence, 6525 North Sheridan Road, Chicago, IL 60626.

PILKINGTON, JAMES PENN, administrator. b. May 3, 1923, Marianna, Arkansas; B.A., Vanderbilt University, 1945; M.A., Vanderbilt University, 1946; administrator, Vanderbilt TV News Archives, Vanderbilt University, 1971 to present. Publication: *The Methodist Publishing House: A History*, 1968. Vanderbilt Television News Archive, Vanderbilt University Library, 419 21st Avenue South, Nashville, TN 37203.

PRATT, GEORGE C., film scholar. b. September 14, 1914, La Grange, Illinois; curator emeritus, department of film, International Museum of Photography at George Eastman House; frequent contributor to *Image*, 1957–1980. Publication: *Spellbound in Darkness*, 1973. P.O. Drawer H, Victor, NY 14564.

PRYLUCK, CALVIN, professor of film. b. January 30, 1924, New York; B.A., New York University, 1952; M.A., University of California at Los

Angeles, 1960; Ph.D., University of Iowa, 1973; professor, department of radio-television-film, Temple University, 1979 to present. Publications: *Structure and Function in Educational Cinema*, 1969; *Sources of Meaning in Motion Pictures and Television*, 1976. Department of Radio-Television-Film, Temple University, Philadelphia, PA 19122.

PRYOR, THOMAS M., editor and journalist. b. May 22, 1912, New York; member of staff, *The New York Times*, 1929–1959; editor, *Daily Variety*, 1959 to present. Daily Variety, 1400 North Cahuenga Boulevard, Hollywood, CA 90028.

QUIRK, LAWRENCE J., writer and critic. b. September 9, 1923, Lynn, Massachusetts; B.A., Suffolk University, 1949; journalist, 1946 to present; editor and publisher of *Quirk's Reviews*, 1972 to present; creator of James R. Quirk Award in memory of his uncle. Publications: *The Films of Joan Crawford*, 1968; *Hobart Francis Kennedy*, 1968; *The Films of Ingrid Bergman*, 1970; *The Films of Paul Newman*, 1971, 1981; *The Films of Fredric March*, 1971; *The Films of William Holden*, 1973, 1986; *The Great Romantic Films*, 1974; *The Films of Robert Taylor*, 1975; *Some Lovely Image*, 1976; *The Films of Ronald Colman*, 1977; *The Films of Warren Beatty*, 1979; *The Films of Myrna Loy*, 1980; *The Films of Gloria Swanson*, 1984; *Claudette Colbert*, 1985; *Lauren Bacall: Her Films and Career*, 1986; *Jane Wyman: The Actress and the Woman*, 1986; *The Complete Films of William Powell*, 1986; *Margaret Sullavan: Child of Fate*, 1986. 74 Charles Street, New York, NY 10014.

RACHOW, LOUIS A., theatre librarian. b. January 21, 1927, Shickley, Nebraska; B.S., York College, 1948; M.L.S., Columbia University, 1959; librarian, Hampden-Booth Theatre Library at the Players Club, 1962 to present; series editor, *Performing Arts Information Guide*, 1975–1982. Publications: *Guide to Performing Arts: 1968*, 1969; *Theatre & Performing Arts Collections*, 1981. 16 Gramercy Park, New York, NY 10003.

RAPF, MAURICE, professor of film and drama. b. May 19, 1914, New York; screenwriter, Hollywood, 1936–1943; staff writer, Walt Disney Productions, 1946–1947; staff writer for various New York companies, 1952–1959; director, 1959–1971; began teaching film theory, writing, and production, Dartmouth College, 1966; taught and launched film studies, Brown University, 1970; adjunct professor of drama and director of film studies, Dartmouth College, 1971–1985; part-time teacher, Dartmouth College, 1985 to present. 6 Conant Road, Hanover, NH 03755.

RENAN, SHELDON, film producer. b. June 29, 1941, Portland, Oregon; B.A., Yale University, 1963; director, Pacific Film Archive, 1968–1974; film producer, 1975 to present; also screenwriter. Publication: *Introduction* *to American Underground Film*, 1967. 1528 Franklin Street, Santa Monica, CA 90404.

RICH, FRANK, theatre critic. b. June 2, 1949, Washington; B.A., Harvard University, 1971; film and TV critic, *Time*, 1977–1980; chief drama critic, *The New York Times*, 1980 to present. The New York Times, 229 West 43 Street, New York, NY 10036.

ROLLINS, PETER C., professor of English and American film studies. b. April 1, 1942, Boston; B.A., Harvard College, 1963; Ph.D., Harvard University, 1972; assistant, associate, and full professor of English and American studies, Oklahoma State University, 1972 to present; producer of film documentaries, *Will Rogers' 1920s: A Cowboy's Guide to the Times*, 1976; *Television's Vietnam: The Impact of Visual Images*, 1983; *Television's Vietnam: The Real Story*, 1985; *Television's Vietnam: The Impact of Media*, 1985; assistant director, *The Writings of Will Rogers* project. Publications: *Benjamin Lee Whorf: Transcendental Linguist*, 1980; *Will Rogers: A Bio-Bibliography*, 1982; *Hollywood as Historian: American Film in a Cultural Context*, 1983. College of Arts and Sciences, 205 Morrill Hall, Stillwater, OK 74078–0135.

SARGENT, RALPH N., III, executive. b. 1941, Lakehurst, New Jersey; B.A., University of North Carolina, 1964; M.A., University of California at Los Angeles, 1965; president and chief executive officer, Film Technology Company, Inc., 1971 to present. Publication: *Preserving the Moving Image*, 1974. 6900 Santa Monica Boulevard, Los Angeles, CA 90038.

SARRIS, ANDREW, film critic and professor of film. b. October 31, 1928, Brooklyn, New York; A.B., Columbia University, 1951; associate editor, *Film Culture*, 1955–1965; film critic, *Village Voice*, 1960 to present; editor-in-chief, *Cahiers du Cinema in English*, 1965–1967; faculty member, Columbia University, school of the arts, 1969 to present; film editor, *Village Voice*, 1975 to present. Publications: *The Films of Josef von Sternberg*, 1966; *Interviews with Film Directors*, 1967; *The Film*, 1968; *The American Cinema: Directors and Directions*, 1929–1968, 1969; *Film 68/69*, co-editor, 1969; *Confessions of a Cultist: On the Cinema*, 1955–1969, 1970; *The Primal Screen: Essays on Film and Related Subjects*, 1972; *The John Ford Movie Mystery*, 1975; *Politics and Cinema*, 1978; *The American Sound Film*, 1987. 19 East 88 Street, New York, NY 10028.

SAUDEK, ROBERT, administrator. b. 1911, Pittsburgh, Pennsylvania; A.B., Harvard University, 1932; chief, motion picture, broadcasting, and recorded sound division, Library of Congress. Library of Congress, Washington, DC 20540.

SCHECHNER, RICHARD, professor of drama. B.A., Cornell University, 1956; M.A., University of Iowa, 1958; Ph.D., Tulane University, 1962; professor of performance studies, New York University, 1967 to present; editor, *The Drama Review*, 1962–1969 and 1985 to present; co-editor, with Brooks McNamara, performance studies series of *Performing Arts Journal*, 1982 to present. Publications: *Public Domain*, 1968; *The Free Southern Theater*, co-editor with Tom Dent, 1968; *Dionysus in 69*, editor, 1970; *Environmental Theater*, 1973; *Theatres, Spaces and Environments*, with Brooks McNamara and Jerry Rojo, 1975; *Essays on Performance Theory*, 1977, 1987; *Ritual, Play, and Performance*, co-editor with Mady Schuman, 1978; *Makbeth*, editor, 1978; *The End of Humanism*, 1982; *Performative Circumstances*, 1983; *La Teoria della Performance*, 1984; *Between Theater and Anthropology*, 1985; *By Means of Performance*, co-editor with Willa Appel, 1987. 249 West 29 Street, New York, NY 10001.

SCHICKEL, RICHARD, writer and film critic. b. February 10, 1933, Milwaukee; B.S., University of Wisconsin, 1955; film critic, *Life*, 1965–1972; film critic, *Time*, 1973 to present. Selected Publications: *The Stars*, 1962; *Movies: The History of an Art and an Institution*, 1964; *The Disney Version*, 1968; *Notes on Some Movies*, 1972; *His Picture in the Papers*, 1974; *Harold Lloyd: The Shape of Laughter*, 1974; *The Men Who Made the Movies*, 1975; *D. W. Griffith: An American Life*, 1984. 311 East 83 Street, New York, NY 10028.

SCHLOSSER, ANNE G., librarian. b. December 28, 1937, New York; B.A., Wheaton College; M.L.S., Simmons College; head, theater arts library, University of California at Los Angeles, 1964–1969; director, Louis B. Mayer Library, American Film Institute, 1969 to present; director, film/TV documentation workshop, American Film Institute, 1977 to present. Publication: *Motion Pictures, Television and Radio: A Union Catalogue of Manuscript and Special Collections in the Western United States*, project director, 1977. 8777 Skyline Drive, Los Angeles, CA 90046.

SENNETT, TED, writer. b. March 20, 1928, Brooklyn, New York; B.A., Brooklyn College, 1948; M.A., Columbia University, 1949. Publications: *Warner Brothers Presents*, 1971; *Lunatics and Lovers*, 1974; *Your Show of Shows*, 1977; *Greenstreet and Lorre: Masters of Menace*, 1979; *Hollywood Musicals*, 1981; *Great Hollywood Movies*, 1983; *Great Movie Directors*, 1986. 31 Patton Lane, Closter, NJ 07624.

SHALE, RICHARD, professor of English. b. January 9, 1947, Youngstown, Ohio; B.A., Ohio Wesleyan University, 1969; M.A., University of Michigan, 1972; Ph.D., University of Michigan, 1976; assistant professor, English department, Youngstown State University, 1981–1985; associate professor, English department, Youngstown State University, 1985 to present. Publications: *Academy Awards: An Ungar Reference Index*, 1978, 1982; *Donald Duck Joins Up: The Walt Disney Studio during World War II*, 1982. English Department, Youngstown State University, Youngstown, OH 44555.

SHALES, TOM, television critic. b. November 3, 1948, Elgin, Illinois; B.A., American University, 1973; TV editor and chief TV critic, *Washington Post*, 1977 to present. Publications: *The American Film Heritage*, editor, 1972; *On the Air!*, 1982. 1150 15th Street N.W., Washington, DC 10071.

SHEEHAN, PATRICK J., film and television librarian. b. January 9, 1939, Great Falls, Montana; B.A., San Francisco State University, 1964; M.L.S., University of California at Berkeley, 1966; head, documentation and reference section, motion picture, broadcasting, and recorded sound division, Library of Congress. Library of Congress, Washington, DC 20540.

SHEPARD, DAVID H., specialist in film. b. October 22, 1940, New York; A.B., Hamilton College, 1962; M.A.C., Annenberg School of Communications, University of Pennsylvania, 1963; associate archivist, American Film Institute, 1968–1973; vice-president for product development, Blackhawk Films, 1973–1976; special projects officer, Directors Guild of America, 1976–1987; lecturer, School of Cinema-TV, University of Southern California, 1982 to present; general editor, Directors Guild of American Oral History series for Scarecrow Press, 1984 to present; producer numerous documentaries. 4236 Klump Avenue, North Hollywood, CA 91602.

SILVER, CHARLES, film curator. b. October 10, 1940, Newark, New Jersey; B.A., Rutgers University, 1962; M.A., Rutgers University, 1964; supervisor, Film Study Center, Museum of Modern Art, New York. Publications: *Marlene Dietrich*, 1974; *The Western Film*, 1976; *Lillian Gish*, 1980; *John Ford*, 1983. Film Study Center, Museum of Modern Art, 11 West 53 Street, New York, NY 10019.

SIMON, JOHN, theatre critic. b. May 12, 1925, Subotica, Yugoslavia; A.B., Harvard University, 1946; A.M., Harvard University, 1948; Ph.D., Harvard University, 1959; theatre critic, *The Hudson Review*, 1960 to present; film critic, *The New Leader*, 1962 to present; theatre critic, *New York*, 1969–1975 and 1977 to present; film critic, *New York*, 1975. Publications: *Acid Test*, 1963; *Private Screenings*, 1967; *Film 67/68*, editor, 1968; *Fourteen for Now*, editor, 1969; *Movies into Film*, 1971; *Ingmar Bergman Directs*, 1972; *Singularities*, 1976; *Uneasy Stages*, 1976; *Reverse Angle*, 1982. 200 East 36 Street, New York, NY 10016.

SIMPSON, MILDRED, librarian. b. March 15, 1939, Bethlehem, Penn-sylvania; B.A., University of Delaware, 1960; M.L.S., University of South-ern California, 1962; librarian, Margaret Herrick Library, Academy of Motion Picture Arts and Sciences, 1964–1978; photography librarian, At-lantic Richfield Company, 1978–1985; graphics librarian, *Los Angeles Times*, 1985 to present. 3122 Butler Avenue, Los Angeles, CA 90066.

SISKEL, GENE, film critic. b. January 26, 1946, Chicago, Illinois; B.A., Yale University, 1967; film critic, *Chicago Tribune*, 1969 to present; co-host, *Sneak Previews*, 1977–1982; co-host, *At the Movies*, 1982–1986; co-host, *Siskel & Ebert & The Movies*, 1986 to present. Chicago Tribune, 435 N. Michigan Avenue, Chicago, IL 60611.

SKLAR, ROBERT, professor of film. b. December 3, 1936, New Bruns-wick, New Jersey; A.B., Princeton, 1958; Ph.D., Harvard, 1965; professor of cinema studies, New York University, 1977 to present. Publications: *F. Scott Fitzgerald: The Last Laocoön*, 1967; *The Plastic Age: 1917–1930*, editor, 1970; *Movie-Made America: A Cultural History of American Movies*, 1975; *Prime-Time America: Life on and behind the Television Screen*, 1980. Depart-ment of Cinema Studies, New York University, 721 Broadway, Room 600, New York, NY 10003.

SLIDE, ANTHONY, film historian. b. November 7, 1944, Birmingham, England; associate archivist, American Film Institute, 1973–1975; resident film historian, Academy of Motion Picture Arts and Sciences, 1975–1980; free-lance film scholar and writer, 1980 to present. Selected Publications: *Early American Cinema*, 1970; *The Films of D. W. Griffith*, with Edward Wagenknecht, 1975; *Early Women Directors*, 1978; *The Vaudevillians*, 1981; *International Film, Radio, and Television Journals*, 1985; *The American Film Industry: A Historical Dictionary*, 1986. 4118 Rhodes Avenue, Studio City, CA 91604.

SMITH, DAVID R., archivist. b. October 13, 1940, Pasadena, California; A.A., Pasadena City College, 1960; B.A., University of California at Berke-ley, 1962; M.L.S., University of California at Berkeley, 1963; archivist, the Walt Disney Company; contributor of monthly column to *Disney Channel Magazine*. Publications: *The Monitor & the Merrimac: A Bibliography*, 1968; *Jack Benny Checklist*, 1970. The Walt Disney Co., 500 S. Buena Vista Street, Burbank, CA 91521.

SPEARS, JACK, film historian and writer. b. December 23, 1919, Fort Smith, Arkansas; B.S., University of Arkansas, 1941; executive director, Tulsa County Medical Society, 1941–1985; editor, *Tulsa Medicine*, 1942–1985; frequent contributor to *Films in Review*, 1955–1977. Publications:

Hollywood: The Golden Era, 1977; *The Civil War on the Screen*, 1977. 354 Utica Square Medical Center, Tulsa, OK 74114.

SPOTO, DONALD, writer. b. June 28, 1941, New Rochelle, New York; B.A., Iona College, 1963; M.A., Fordham University, 1966; Ph.D., Fordham University, 1970; member of faculty, New School for Social Research, 1975 to present. Publications: *The Art of Alfred Hitchcock*, 1976; *Camerado*, 1978; *Stanley Kramer, Film Maker*, 1978; *The Dark Side of Genius*, 1983; *The Kindness of Strangers*, 1985; *Falling in Love Again*, 1985. c/o Little Brown & Co., 34 Beacon Street, Boston, MA 02106.

STAIGER, JANET, professor of film. b. October 8, 1946, Omaha, Nebraska; B.A., University of Nebraska at Omaha, 1968; M.A., Purdue University, 1969; Ph.D., University of Wisconsin at Madison, 1981; assistant professor, department of cinema studies, New York University, 1983 to present. Publications: *Film Studies Annual*, co-editor with Ben Lawton, 1976; *Film Studies Annual*, co-editor with Ben Lawton, 1977; *The Classical Hollywood Cinema: Film Style and Mode of Production to 1960*, with David Bordwell and Kristin Thompson, 1985. 1 Washington Square Village, #16K, New York, NY 10012.

STAPLES, DONALD E., professor of film and television. b. April 15, 1934, Brooklyn, New York; B.S., Northwestern University, 1955; M.A., University of Southern California, 1959; Ph.D., Northwestern University, 1967; professor of cinema, New York University, 1969–1980; professor of film and television, North Texas State University, 1979 to present; chairman, department of radio, television and film, North Texas State University, 1979–1986. Publications: *Copyrighting of Motion Pictures: History and Present Procedures*, 1959; *A Statistical Study of Award-Winning American Films and Their Makers, 1930–1964*, 1967; *Film Encounter*, with R. Hector Currie, 1973; *American Cinema*, editor, 1974. 2901 Montecito Road, Denton, TX 76205.

STERLING, CHRISTOPHER H., professor of communication. b. April 16, 1943, Washington, D.C.; B.S., University of Wisconsin, 1965; M.S., University of Wisconsin, 1967; Ph.D., University of Wisconsin, 1969; professor of communications, Temple University, 1970–1980; special assistant to Federal Communications Commissioner Anne P. Jones, 1980–1982; director, Center for Telecommunication Studies, George Washington University, 1982–1984; program director, telecommunications policy program, graduate school of arts and sciences, George Washington University, 1984 to present; founder and editor-publisher, *Communication Booknotes*, 1969 to present; editor, *Telecommunications Update*, 1985 to present. Publications: *Mass News: Practices, Controversies, Alternatives*, with D. LeRoy, 1973; *Stay*

Tuned: A Concise History of American Broadcasting, with J. Kittross, 1978, 1987; *The Mass Media*, with T. Haight, 1978; *Who Owns the Media?*, co-author, 1982; *International Telecommunications and Information Policy*, editor, 1984; *Electronic Media: A Guide to Trends in Broadcasting and Newer Technologies, 1920–1983*, 1984; *Decision To Divest: Major Documents in U.S. v AT&T, 1974–1984*, co-editor, 1986; *Broadcasting in America: A Survey of Electronic Media*, co-author, 1987. 4507 Airlie Way, Annandale, VA 22003.

STEVENS, GEORGE, JR., administrator and film maker. b. April 3, 1932, Hollywood, California; B.A., Occidental College, 1953; director of the motion picture and television service of the United States Information Agency, 1962–1967; founding director, American Film Institute, 1967–1979; life trustee and co-chairman of the board, American Film Institute, 1979 to present; executive producer, American Film Institute Life Achievement Award television presentation, 1973 to present; co-producer, Kennedy Center Honors programs, 1978 to present; executive producer, *Christmas in Washington*, 1982 to present; director, producer and writer, *George Stevens: A Filmmaker's Journey*, 1985. Third Floor, Kennedy Center, Washington, DC 20566.

SULLIVAN, DAN, theatre critic. b. October 22, 1935, Worcester, Massachusetts; A.B., Holy Cross College, 1957; drama critic, *Los Angeles Times*, 1969 to present. Los Angeles Times, Times Mirror Square, Los Angeles, CA 90053.

SWERDLOVE, DOROTHY L., librarian. b. January 4, 1928, New York; B.A., Swarthmore College, 1948; M.L.S., Columbia University, 1961; first assistant, Billy Rose theatre collection, New York Public Library, 1967–1980; curator, Billy Rose theatre collection, New York Public Library, 1980 to present. Billy Rose Theatre Collection, New York Public Library at Lincoln Center, 111 Amsterdam Avenue, New York, NY 10023.

TERRACE, VINCENT, television and radio historian. b. May 14, 1948, New York; B.F.A., New York Institute of Technology, 1971; Publications: *The Complete Encyclopedia of Television Programs, 1947–1976*, 1976; *The Complete Encyclopedia of Television Programs, 1947–1979*, 1979; *Radio's Golden Years, 1930–1960*, 1980; *Television 1970–1980*, 1981; *Actors' TV Credits, Supplement II, 1977–1981*, 1982; *Encyclopedia of Television Series, Pilots and Specials, 1974–1984*, 1985; *Encyclopedia of Television Series, Pilots and Specials, 1937–1973*, 1986. 1830 Delancey Place, Bronx, NY 10462.

THOMAS, BOB, writer and journalist. b. January 26, 1922, San Diego, California; Hollywood columnist, Associated Press, 1944 to present; editor, *Action*, 1968–1974. Selected Publications: *Walt Disney: The Art of Animation*,

1958; *Thalberg: Life and Legend*, 1969; *Selznick*, 1970; *Marlon: Portrait of the Rebel as an Artist*, 1973; *Joan Crawford*, 1978; *Golden Boy: The Untold Story of William Holden*, 1983; *Astaire, the Man, the Dancer*, 1984; *I Got Rhythm!: The Ethel Merman Story*, 1985. 16509 Adlon Road, Encino, CA 91436.

THOMPSON, KRISTIN, film professor. b. April 4, 1950, Iowa City, Iowa; B.A., University of Iowa, 1971; M.A., University of Iowa, 1973; Ph.D., University of Wisconsin at Madison, 1977; honorary fellowship, University of Wisconsin at Madison, department of communication arts, 1982–1987. Publications: *Film Art: An Introduction*, with David Bordwell, 1979; *Eisenstein's Ivan the Terrible: A Neoreformalist Analysis*, 1981; *The Classical Hollywood Cinema*, with David Bordwell and Janet Staiger, 1985; *Exporting Entertainment: America in the World Film Market, 1907–1934*, 1985. 544 S. Owen Drive, Madison, WI 53711.

TOLL, ROBERT C., writer. b. September 10, 1938, San Francisco; B.A., California State University at San Jose, 1964; M.A., University of California at Berkeley, 1964; Ph.D., University of California at Berkeley, 1966. Publications: *Blacking Up: The Minstrel Show in Nineteenth Century America*, 1974; *Old Slack's Reminiscences and Pocket History of the Colored Profession*, co-editor, 1974; *On with the Show: The First Century of Show Business in America*, 1976; *The Entertainment Machine: American Show Business in the Twentieth Century*, 1982. 3900 Harrison Street, Apt. 203, Oakland, CA.

TURNER, GEORGE E., writer and editor. b. September 30, 1925, Burk Burnett, Texas; B.A., West Texas State University, 1950; member of staff, American Society of Cinematographers, 1982 to present; editor, *American Cinematographer*, 1985 to present. Selected Publications: *The Making of King Kong*, with Orville Goldner, 1975; *Forgotten Horrors*, with Michael H. Price, 1978; *The ASC Treasury of Visual Effects*, with Linwood G. Dunn, 1983. P.O. Box 2230, Hollywood, CA 90078.

TUSKA, JON, writer. b. April 30, 1942, Milwaukee; A.B., Marquette University, 1966; founder and editor, *Views & Reviews*, 1969–1975; producer, writer, and host, PBS series, "They Went Thataway," 1969–1971; member of adjunct faculty, Lewis & Clark College, 1979 to present. Publications: *Philo Vance: The Life and Times of S. S. Van Dine*, 1973; *The Films of Mae West*, 1973; *The Filming of the West*, 1976; *Close-Up: The Contract Director*, 1976; *The Detective in Hollywood*, 1978; *Close-Up: The Hollywood Director*, 1978; *Close-Up: The Contemporary Director*, 1981; *The Vanishing Legion: A History of Mascot Pictures, 1927–1935*, 1982; *The American West in Fiction*, 1982; *Encyclopedia of Frontier and Western Fiction*, with Vicki Piekarski, 1983; *Billy the Kid: A Bio-Bibliography*, 1983; *The Frontier Experience*, with Vicki Piekarski, 1984; *Dark Cinema: American Film Noir in Cultural*

Perspective, 1984; *The American West in Film: Critical Approaches to the Western*, 1985; *In Manors and Alleys: A Casebook on the American Detective Film*, 1988. 3318 S.E. Madison, Portland, OR 97214.

VOGEL, AMOS, professor of film. b. April 18, 1921, Vienna, Austria; B.A., New School of Social Research, 1949; Hon. M.A., University of Pennsylvania, 1975; former columnist, *Village Voice* and *Film Comment*; professor of film, Annenberg School of Communications, University of Pennsylvania, 1974 to present. Publication: *Film as a Subversive Art*, 1974. 15 Washington Place, New York, NY 10003.

WAGENKNECHT, EDWARD, writer and critic. b. March 28, 1900, Chicago; Ph.B., University of Chicago, 1923; M.A., University of Chicago, 1924; Ph.D., University of Washington, 1932; professor of English emeritus, Boston University; author of more than 60 books. Selected Publications: *Lillian Gish: An Interpretation*, 1927; *Geraldine Farrar, An Authorized Record of Her Career*, 1929; *A Guide to Bernard Shaw*, 1929, 1971; *Jenny Lind*, 1931, 1980; *The Movies in the Age of Innocence*, 1962; *Seven Daughters of the Theater*, 1964; *Merely Players*, 1966; *The Films of D. W. Griffith*, with Anthony Slide, 1975; *Fifty Great American Silent Films, 1912–1920*, with Anthony Slide, 1980. 233 Otis Street, West Newton, MA 02165.

WAGNER, ROBERT W., professor of film, television, and mass communication. b. November 16, 1918, Newport News, Virginia; B.Sc., Ohio State University, 1940; M.A., Ohio State University, 1941; Ph.D., Ohio State University, 1953; member of board of directors, American Film Institute, 1974–1981; professor emeritus, Ohio State University; professor of mass communication and film, Emerson College. Publications: *Series of Motion Picture Documents on Communication Theory and New Educational Media*, 1966; *Education of Film Maker*, 1975. 1353 Zollinger Road, Upper Arlington, OH 43221.

WANAMAKER, MARC, film researcher and writer. b. October 1, 1947, Hollywood, California; A.A., Los Angeles City College, 1968; B.A., University of California at Northridge, 1971; founder and owner, Bison Archives, specializing in research on the motion picture studios of the United States. 1600 Schuyler Road, Beverly Hills, CA 90210.

WATT, DOUGLAS, theatre critic. b. January 20, 1914, New York; A.B., Cornell University, 1934; staff writer, *The New Yorker*, 1946 to present; senior drama critic, New York *Daily News*, 1971 to present. 27 West 86 Street, New York, NY 10024.

WEALES, GERALD, professor of English. b. June 12, 1925, Connersville, Indiana; A.B., Columbia University, 1948; A.M., Columbia University, 1949; Ph.D., Columbia University, 1958; professor of English, University of Pennsylvania, 1967 to present. Selected Publications: *Religion in Modern English Drama*, 1961; *American Drama since World War II*, 1962; *Edwardian Plays*, editor, 1962; *The Jumping-Off Place: American Drama in the 1960's*, 1969; *Clifford Odets, Playwright*, 1971; *Canned Goods as Caviar: American Film Comedy of the 1930's*, 1985. Department of English, University of Pennsylvania, Philadelphia, PA 19104.

WELSH, JAMES M., professor of English and film. b. July 15, 1938, Logansport, Indiana; B.A., Indiana University, 1963; M.A., University of Kansas, 1965; associate professor of English and film, Salisbury State College, 1971 to present; arts editor and reviewer, WBOC-TV, 1980 to present; co-founder and editor, *Literature/Film Quarterly*, 1973 to present. Publications: *Ben Johnson: A Quadricentennial Bibliography, 1947–1972*, with D. H. Brock, 1974; *His Majesty the American: The Films of Douglas Fairbanks, Sr.*, with John C. Tibbetts, 1977; *Abel Gance*, with Steven P. Kramer, 1978; *Peter Watkins: A Guide to References and Resources*, 1986. English Department, Salisbury State College, Salisbury, MD 21801.

WILLIAMSON, BRUCE, film critic. b. December 31, 1930, Michigan; film critic, *Time*, 1963–1966; film critic, *Playboy*, 1967 to present. Playboy, 919 North Michigan Avenue, Chicago, IL 60611.

WILLIS, DONALD C., film critic and historian. b. September 18, 1947, Santa Barbara, California; B.A., University of California at Los Angeles, 1969. Publications: *The Films of Frank Capra*, 1974; *The Films of Howard Hawks*, 1975; *Horror & Science Fiction Films*, Vol. I, 1972, Vol. II, 1982, Vol. III, 1984; *Variety's Complete Science Fiction Reviews*, editor, 1985. 2410 Dwight Way, #3, Berkeley, CA 94704.

WILLIS, JOHN, editor. b. October 16, 1916, Morristown, Tennessee; B.A., Milligan College, 1938; M.A., University of Tennessee, 1941; assistant editor, *Theatre World*, 1945–1965; assistant editor, *Screen World*, 1948–1965; editor, *Theatre World*, 1965 to present; editor, *Screen World*, 1965 to present; editor, *Dance World*, 1966–1980. 190 Riverside Drive, New York, NY 10024.

WILMETH, DON B., professor of theatre arts and English. b. December 15, 1939, Houston, Texas; B.A., Abilene Christian University, 1961; M.A., University of Arkansas, 1962; Ph.D., University of Illinois, 1964; professor of theatre arts and English, Brown University, 1967 to present. Publications: *American Stage to World War I*, 1978; *George Frederick Cooke: Machiavel of* *the Stage*, 1980; *American and English Popular Entertainment*, 1980; *The Language of American Popular Entertainment*, 1981; *Variety Entertainment and Outdoor Amusements*, 1982; *Plays by William Gillette*, co-editor, 1983; *Plays by Augustin Daly*, co-editor, 1984; *Cambridge Guide to World Theatre*, advisory editor, 1987. Department of Theatre, Speech, and Dance, Brown University, Box 1897, Providence, RI 02912.

WOLF, WILLIAM, film critic. b. Somerville, New Jersey; film critic, *Cue*, 1964–1980; lecturer in film, New York University, 1980 to present; contributing editor, *New York*, 1980 to present. Publications: *The Marx Brothers*, 1976; *Landmark Films: The Cinema and Our Century*, with Lillian Wolf, 1979. 155 West 68 Street, New York, NY 10023.

WOODS, ALAN L., professor of theatre history. b. November 23, 1942; A.B., Columbia University, 1964; M.A., Columbia University, 1969; Ph.D., University of Southern California, 1972; associate professor, department of theatre, Ohio State University, 1972 to present; director, Jerome Lawrence and Robert E. Lee Theatre Research Institute, Ohio State University, 1979 to present. Publication: *The Ohio Theatre, 1928–1978*, 1979. 198 Walhalla Road, Columbus, OH 43202.

Useful Addresses

Bookshops

The following is a list of major bookstores specializing in film and theatre located in English speaking countries:

AUSTRALIA

Gaumont Book Company
123 Little Collins Street
Melbourne, Victoria 3000
(03) 663–2623

Readings Records and Books
132d Toorak Road
South Yarra, Victoria 3141
(03) 267–1885

Soft Focus
P.O. Box 98
Ringwood East
Victoria 3135

Space Age Books
305–307 Swanston Street
Melbourne, Victoria 3000
(03) 663–1777

CANADA

Broadway and Hollywood Books
17 Yorkville Avenue
Toronto
Canada M4X 1L1
(416) 926–8992

Theatrebooks
25 Bloor Street W
Toronto
Canada M4W 1A3
(416) 922–7175

UNITED KINGDOM

A. E. Cox
21 Cecil Road
Itchen
Southampton SO2 7HX
(0703) 447–989

Anne FitzSimmons
The Retreat, The Green
Wetheral
Carlisle, Cumbria CA4 8ET
(0228) 60 675

A. Zwemmer, Ltd.
78 Charing Cross Road
London WC2
(01) 836–4710

The Cinema Bookshop
13–14 Great Russell Street
London WC1
(01) 637–0206

The Cinema Shop
Filmhouse
88 Lothian Road
Edinburgh EH3 9B2
(031) 228 6382

Cine-Search
24 Cranbourne Street
London WC2H 7 AA

C. Sutherland
15 Aldridge Road Village
London W11 1BL
(01) 221–0091

The Motion Picture Bookshop
National Film Theatre
South Bank
London SE1
(01) 928–3517

Motley Books
Montisfont Abbey
Romsey
Hampshire SO5 OLP

Movie Finds
4 Ravenslea Road
Balham
London SW12 8SB
(01) 673–6534

Movies
36 Meon Road
London W3 8AN
(01) 993–2859

Peter Wood
20 Stonehill Road
Great Shelford
Cambridge GB2 5JL
(0223) 842 419

That's Entertainment
43 The Market
Covent Garden
London WC2E 8RG
(01) 240–3490

Treasures & Pleasures of Past Times
11 Cecil Court
Charing Cross Road
London WC2H 7JS
(01) 734–0795

Vintage Magazine Co., Ltd.
39–41 Brewer Street
London W1
(01) 836–4710

UNITED STATES

Aladdin Books and Memorabilia
122 West Commonwealth Avenue
Fullerton, CA 92632
(714) 738–6115

Birns & Sawyer, Inc.
1026 N. Highland Avenue
Hollywood, CA 90038
(213) 466–8211

Book Castle
200 North Golden Mall
Burbank, CA 91502
(818) 845–9150

Book City
6625 Hollywood Boulevard
Hollywood, CA 90028
(213) 466–1049

The Book Sail
1186 North Tustin Street
Orange, CA 92667
(714) 997–9511

Cinemabilia
611 Broadway, Suite 203
New York, NY 10012
(212) 533–6686

Cinema Books
701 Broadway East
Seattle, WA 98102
(206) 547–7667

Cinema Books by Post
P.O. Box 20092, Broadway Station
Seattle, WA 98102

Dayton's Record Store
824 Broadway at 12th Street
New York, NY 10003
(212) 254–5084

Drama Books
511 Geary Street
San Francisco, CA 94102
(415) 441–5343

Drama Bookshop
723 Seventh Avenue
New York, NY 10019
(212) 944–0595

Elliot M. Katt Performing Arts Books
8568 Melrose Avenue
Los Angeles, CA 90069
(213) 652–5178

Four Continent Book Corporation
149 Fifth Avenue
New York, NY 10010
(212) 533–0250

Gotham Book Mart
41 West 47th Street
New York, NY 10036
(212) 719–4448

Herbert Linder
55 Park Avenue
New York, NY 10016
(212) 685–2571

J-N Herlin
68 Thompson Street
New York, NY 10012
(212) 431–8732

Larry Edmunds Bookshop
6658 Hollywood Blvd.
Hollywood, CA 90028
(213) 463–3273

Larry Edmunds Bookshop
11969 Ventura Blvd.
Studio City, CA 91604
(818) 508–7511

Limelight Bookstore
1803 Market Street
San Francisco, CA 94103
(415) 864–2265

Richard Stoddard
90 East Tenth Street
New York, NY 10003
(212) 982–9440

Samuel French Theatre Bookshop
7623 West Sunset Blvd.
Los Angeles, CA 90046
(213) 876–0570

Samuel French Theatre Bookshop
45 West 25th Street
New York, NY 10010
(212) 206–8990

Samuel French Theatre Bookshop
11963 Ventura Blvd.
Studio City, CA 91604
(818) 762–0535

Strand Book Store
828 Broadway
New York, NY 10003
(212) 473–1452

Theatre Books
1576 Broadway
New York, NY 10036
(212) 757–2834

Theatricana, Inc.
Box 4244
Campus Station
Athens, GA 30602
(404) 548–2514

Journals and Magazines ⎯⎯⎯⎯

This listing is limited to English-language publications.

American Cinematographer
The American Society of Cinematographers
1782 N. Orange Drive
Hollywood, CA 90028

American Film
3 East 54th Street
New York, NY 10022

American Premiere
8421 Wilshire Blvd., Suite 205
Beverly Hills, CA 90211

Applause
San Diego Applause Magazine, Inc.
454 Olive Street
San Diego, CA 92103

Back Stage
Backstage Publications, Inc.
165 West 46th Street
New York, NY 10036

The Big Reel
Empire Publishing, Inc.
Route 3
Madison, NC 27025

Billboard
1515 Broadway
New York, NY 10036

Boxoffice Magazine
RLD Publishing Corp.
1800 N. Highland Avenue, Suite 316
Hollywood, CA 90028

Broadcasting
Broadcasting Publications, Inc.
1735 DeSales Street NW
Washington, DC 20036

Broadcast Week
Titsch Communications, Inc.
Box 5727-TA
2500 Curtis Street, Suite 200
Denver, CO 80205

Canadian Theatre Review
York University
Downsview, ONT M3J 1P3
Canada

Cantrill's Filmnotes
Box 1295L
G.P.O. Melbourne, Victoria 3001
Australia

Channels
CC Publishing Inc.
19 West 44th Street
New York, NY 10036

Children's Theatre Review
American Theatre Association
1000 Vermont Avenue NW
Washington, DC 20005

Cineaste
200 Park Avenue South
New York, NY 10003

Cinefantastique
Frederick S. Clark
P.O. Box 270
Oak Park, IL 60303

Cinefex
P.O. Box 20027
Riverside, CA 92516

Cinema Journal
Society for Cinema Studies
Department of English
University of Illinois at Chicago
Chicago, IL 60680

Cinema Papers
644 Victoria Street
North Melbourne, Victoria 3051
Australia

Classic Images
Muscatine Journal
P.O. Box 809
Muscatine, IA 52761

Communication Booknotes
George Washington University
Department of Communication and Theatre
Washington, DC 20052

Comparative Drama
Western Michigan University
Kalamazoo, MI 49008–3899

Daily Variety
1400 N. Cahuenga Blvd.
Hollywood, CA 90028

Dial Magazine
Public Broadcasting Communications, Inc.
304 West 58th Street
New York, NY 10019

Drama-Logue
P.O. Box 38771
Los Angeles, CA 90038–0771

Drama Review
New York University School of the Arts
51 West Fourth Street
New York, NY 10012

Dramatics
International Thespian Society
3368 Central Parkway
Cincinnati, OH 45225

Dramatists Guild Quarterly
Dramatists Guild, Inc.
234 West 44th Street
New York, NY 10036

Emmy
Academy of Television Arts and Sciences
3500 West Olive Avenue, Suite 700
Burbank, CA 91505

Encore
1st Floor
41A The Corso
Manly, New South Wales 2095
Australia

Entertainment Law Journal
Larry A. Thompson Organization
1888 Century Park East, Suite 622
Los Angeles, CA 90067

Entertainment Law Reporter
Entertainment Law Publishing Company
9440 Santa Monica Blvd., Suite 600
Beverly Hills, CA 90210

Essays in Theatre
Department of Drama
University of Guelph
Guelph, Ontario N1G 2WI
Canada

Film
British Federation of Film Societies
81 Dean Street
London W1V 6AA
England

Film & History
New Jersey Institute of Technology
Newark, NJ 07102

Film Bulletin
Wax Publications, Inc.
1239 Vine Street
Philadelphia, PA 19107

Film Comment
140 West 65th Street
New York, NY 10023

Film Criticism
Allegheny College
Meadville, PA 16335

Film Dope
40 Willifield Way
London NW11 7XT
England

Film Journal
244 West 49th Street, Suite 305
New York, NY 10019

Film Quarterly
University of California Press
Berkeley, CA 94720

Films and Filming
Brevert Publishing, Ltd.
145–147 North End
Croyden, Surrey CR0 1TN
England

Films in Review
National Board of Review of Motion Pictures, Inc.
P.O. Box 589
New York, NY 10021

Framework
University of East Anglia
Norwich NR4 7TJ
England

The Historical Journal of Film, Radio & Television
Carfax Publishing Company
P.O. Box 25
Abingdon, Oxfordshire OX14 1RW
England

The Hollywood Reporter
6715 Sunset Blvd.
Hollywood, CA 90028

Hollywood Studio Magazine
3960 Laurel Canyon Blvd., Suite 450
Studio City, CA 91604

Home Viewer
11 N. 2nd Street
Philadelphia, PA 19106

Horizon
Boone, Inc.
Drawer 30
Tuscaloosa, AL 35402

Image
International Museum of Photography at
George Eastman House
900 East Avenue
Rochester, NY 14607

The International Photographer
Local 659
7715 Sunset Boulevard
Hollywood, CA 90046

Journal of Broadcasting & Electronic Media
1771 N Street NW
Washington, DC 20036

Journal of Film and Video
University Film and Video Association
Department of Communication Arts and Sciences
Rosary College
7900 West Division Street
River Forrest, IL 60305

Journal of Popular Film and Television
Heldref Publications
4000 Albemarle Street
Washington, DC 20016

Jump Cut: A Review of Contemporary Cinema
P.O. Box 865
Berkeley, CA 94701

Literature/Film Quarterly
Salisbury State College
Salisbury, MD 21801

Loyola Entertainment Law Journal
Loyola Law School
1441 West Olympic Blvd.
Los Angeles, CA 90015

Millimeter
826 Broadway
New York, NY 10003

Monthly Film Bulletin
The British Film Institute
81 Dean Street
London W1V 6AA
England

Movie Collector's World
151 E. Birch Street
Annandale, MN 55302

Movie/TV Marketing
Box 30
Central Post Office
Tokyo, 100–91
Japan

Newsreel
1 Governors Lane
Shelburne, VT 05481

New York Theatre Critics' Reviews
Proscenium Publications
4 Park Avenue
New York, NY 10016

On Cable
On Cable Publications
25 Van Zant Street
Norwalk, CT 06855

On Location
6777 Hollywood Blvd.
Hollywood, CA 90038

Performance
1020 Currie Street
Fort Worth, TX 76107

Performing Arts
2999 Overland Avenue, Suite 201
Los Angeles, CA 90064

Performing Arts in Canada
52 Avenue Road, Second Floor
Toronto, Ontario M5R 2G2
Canada

Playbill
Playbill, Inc.
71 Vanderbilt Avenue
New York, NY 10169

Plays and Players
Brevet Publishing, Ltd.
145–147 North End
Croydon, Surrey CR0 1TN
England

Post Script
Jacksonville University
Jacksonville, FL 32211

Pre-vue
P.O. Box 31255
Billings, MT 59107

Quarterly Review of Film Studies
Redgrave Publishing Company
360 Adams Street
Bedford Hills, NY 10507

Quirk's Reviews
74 Charles Street
New York, NY 10014

Restoration and 16th Century Theatre Research
Loyola University of Chicago
6525 North Sheridan Road
Chicago, IL 60626

Screen
Society for Education in Film and Television, Ltd.
29 Old Compton Street
London W1V 5PL
England

Screen International
King Publications, Ltd.
Kingscreen House
6–7 Great Chapel Street
London W1V 4BR
England

Sequences
4005 rue de Bellechasse
Montreal, Quebec H1X 1J6
Canada

The Shakespeare Newsletter
1217 Ashland Avenue
Evanston, IL 60202

Shakespeare Quarterly
Folger Shakespeare Library
201 East Capitol Street S.E.
Washington, DC 20003

Sight and Sound
The British Film Institute
127 Charing Cross Road
London WC2 0EA
England

Sightlines
Educational Film Library Association, Inc.
45 John Street, Suite 301
New York, NY 10038

SMPTE Journal
Society of Motion Picture and Television Engineers, Inc.
595 West Hartsdale Avenue
White Plains, NY 10607–1824

Soap Opera Digest
SOD Publishing, Inc.
254 West 31st Street
New York, NY 10001

Theatre
Yale University
School of Drama
222 York Street
Yale Station
New Haven, CT 06520

Theatre
41 West 72nd Street, 14 G
New York, NY 10023

Theatre Communications
Theatre Communications Group
355 Lexington Avenue
New York, NY 10017

Theatre Crafts Magazine
Theatre Crafts Association
135 5th Avenue
New York, NY 10010

Theatre Journal
American Theatre Association
1010 Wisconsin Avenue NW
Washington, DC 20007

Theatre News
American Theatre Association
1010 Wisconsin Avenue NW
Washington, DC 20007

Theatre Notebook
Society for Theatre Research
77 Kinnerton Street
London SW1 8ED
England

Theatre Organ
American Theatre Organ Society, Inc.
4429 Pennsylvania Avenue
Fair Oaks, CA 95628

Theatre Research International
Oxford University Press
Walton Street
Oxford, OX2 6OP
England

TV Guide
Triangle Publications
4 Radnor Corporate Center
Radnor, PA 19088

Variety
154 West Fifty-Sixth Street
New York, NY 10022

VCR, Home Video Monthly
9509 U.S. Highway 42
P.O. Box 385
Prospect, KY 40059

Videography
United Business Publications, Inc.
475 Park Avenue South
New York, NY 10016

Video Review Magazine
Viare Publishing
902 Broadway
New York, NY 10010

Video Times Magazine
Publications International, Ltd.
3841 West Oakton Street
Skokie, IL 60076

Wide Angle
Ohio University
Department of Film
College of Fine Arts,
The Athens Center for Film and Video
Box 388
Athens, OH 45701

Specialist Publishers _____

The following is a list of major publishers and/ or distributors of books on the performing arts in the United States.

Chadwyck-Healey, Inc.
1101 King Street
Alexandria, VA 22314
(703) 683–4890

Citadel Press
120 Enterprise Avenue
Secaucus, NJ 07094
(201) 866–4199

Columbia University Press
562 West 113 Street
New York, NY 10025
(212) 316–7100

Communications Press, Inc.
1346 Connecticut Avenue NW
Washington, DC 20036
(202) 785–0865

Crown Publishers, Inc.
1 Park Avenue
New York, NY 10016
(212) 254–1600

Da Capo Press, Inc.
233 Spring Street
New York, NY 10013
(212) 620–8000

Dover Publications, Inc
180 Varick Street
New York, NY 10014
(212) 255–3755

Drama Book Publishers
821 Broadway
New York, NY 10003
(212) 228–3400

The Dramatics Publishing Co.
Box 109
311 Washington Street
Woodstock, IL 60098
(815) 338–7170

Dramatists Play Service, Inc.
440 Park Avenue South
New York, NY 10016
(212) 683–8960

Farrar, Straus and Giroux, Inc.
19 Union Square West
New York, NY 10003
(212) 741–6900

Focal Press
80 Montvale Avenue
Stoneham, MA 02180
(617) 438–8464

Gale Research Company
Book Tower
Detroit, MI 48226
(313) 961–2242

Garland Publishing, Inc.
136 Madison Avenue
New York, NY 10016
(212) 686–7492

Greenwood Press, Inc.
Box 5007
Westport, CT 06881
(203) 226–3571

Hastings House Publishers, Inc.
10 East 40 Street
New York, NY 10016
(212) 689–5400

Lyle Stuart, Inc.
120 Enterprise Avenue
Secaucus, NJ 07094
(201) 866–0490

McFarland & Company, Inc.
Box 611
Jefferson, NC 28640
(919) 246–4460

New York Zoetrope, Inc.
80 East 11 Street
New York, NY 10003
(212) 420–0590

Oryx Press
2214 North Central Avenue
Phoenix, AZ 85004
(602) 254–6156

Oxford University Press, Inc.
200 Madison Avenue
New York, NY 10016
(212) 679–7300

Players Press
Box 1132
4264 Fulton Avenue
Studio City, CA 91604
(818) 789–4980

Plays, Inc.
120 Boylston Street
Boston, MA 02116
(617) 423–3157

Redgrave Publishing Co.
380 Adams Street
Bedford Hills, NY 10507
(914) 241–7100

R. R. Bowker Co.
205 East 42 Street
New York, NY 10017
(212) 916–1600

Salem Press, Inc.
P.O. Box 1097
Englewood Cliffs, NJ 07632
(201) 871–3700

Samuel French, Inc.
45 West 25 Street
New York, NY 10010
(212) 206–8990

Simon & Schuster, Inc.
1230 Avenue of the Americas
New York, NY 10020
(212) 245–6400

Tab Books, Inc.
Blue Ridge Summit, PA 17214
(717) 794–2191

Theatre Arts Books
153 Waverly Place
New York, NY 10014
(212) 675–8815

Theatre Communications Group
355 Lexington Avenue
New York, NY 10017
(212) 697–5230

Twayne Publishers
70 Lincoln Street
Boston, MA 02111
(617) 423–3990

UMI Research Press
300 North Zeeb Road
P.O. Box 1467
Ann Arbor, MI 48106
(313) 761–4700

University Microfilms International
300 North Zeeb Road
P.O. Box 1467
Ann Arbor, MI 48106
(313) 761–4700

University of California Press, Inc.
2223 Fulton Street
Berkeley, CA 94720
(415) 642–4247

University Publications of America
44 North Market Street
Frederick, MD 21701
(301) 694–0100

Organizations

The following listing provides names, addresses, and telephone numbers for organizations, guilds, unions, associations, and institutions in all areas of the performing arts.

Academy of Canadian Cinema
653 Yonge Street, 2nd Floor
Toronto, Ontario M4Y 1Z9
Canada
(416) 967–0315

Academy of Motion Picture Arts and Sciences
8949 Wilshire Boulevard
Beverly Hills, CA 90211
(213) 127–8990

Academy of Television Arts and Sciences
3500 West Olive Avenue, Suite 700
Burbank, CA 91505
(818) 953–7575

Action for Children's Television
46 Austin Street
Newtonville, MA 02160
(617) 527–7870

Actors Equity Association
165 West 46 Street
New York, NY 10036
(212) 869–8530

Actors Fund of America
1501 Broadway
New York, NY 10036
(212) 869–8530

Actors Fund of America Home
155 West Hudson Avenue
Englewood, NJ 07631
(201) 894–9523

Adult Film Association of America
1654 Cordova Street
Los Angeles, CA 90007
(213) 731–7236

Advanced TV Systems Committee
155 West 68 Street, Suite 35F
New York, NY 10023
(212) 293–3546

The Advertising Council
825 Third Avenue
New York, NY 10022
(212) 758–0400

Affiliate Artists
158 West 68 Street
New York, NY 10023
(212) 580–2000

Affiliated Property Craftsmen
Local 44 (IATSE)
7429 Sunset Boulevard
Hollywood, CA 90046
(213) 876–2320

Afro-American Studio Theatre
415 West 127 Street
New York, NY 10027

Afro-American Total Theatre
c/o Empire Hotel
44 West 63 Street
New York, NY 10023

Alliance for Gay and Lesbian Artists in the Entertainment Industry
P.O. Box 69A18
Los Angeles, CA 90069
(213) 273–7199

Alliance of Canadian Cinema, Television and Radio Artists
2239 Yonge Street
Toronto, Ontario M4S 2B5
Canada
(416) 489–1311

Alliance of Motion Picture & TV Producers
14144 Ventura Boulevard
Sherman Oaks, CA 91423
(818) 995–3600

Alliance of Resident Theatres/New York
325 Spring Street, Room 315
New York, NY 10013
(212) 989–5257

Alpha Psi Omega
c/o Dr. Yetta G. Mitchell
P.O. Box 322
Waxahachie, TX 75165
(214) 937–3062

American Academy and Institute of Arts and Letters
633 West 155 Street
New York, NY 10032
(212) 368–5900

American Academy of Dramatic Arts
120 Madison Avenue
New York, NY 10016
(212) 686–9244

American Arts Alliance, Inc.
424 C Street, NE
Washington, DC 20002
(202) 544–3900

American Association of Cable Television Owners
Downtown Station 883
Atlanta, GA 30303
(404) 681–0797

American Center of Films for Children
School of Cinema/TV
University of Southern California
Los Angeles, CA 90089
(213) 743–8632

American Cinema Editors
4416½ Finley Avenue
Los Angeles, CA 90027
(213) 660–4425

American College Theatre Festival
John F. Kennedy Center for the Performing Arts
Washington, DC 20566
(202) 254–3437

American Community Theatre Association
1000 Vermont Avenue NW, Suite 902
Washington, DC 20005
(202) 737–5606

American Council for the Arts
570 Seventh Avenue
New York, NY 10018
(212) 354–6655

American Federation of Film Societies
3 Washington Square Village
New York, NY 10012
(212) 254–8688

American Federation of Musicians (AFL-CIO)
1501 Broadway
New York, NY 10036
(212) 869–1330

American Federation of Television and Radio Artists (AFTRA)
1350 Avenue of the Americas
New York, NY 10019
(212) 265–7700

American Federation of Television and Radio Artists (AFTRA)
1717 North Highland Avenue
Hollywood, CA 90028
(213) 461–8111

American Federation of the Arts
41 East 65 Street
New York, NY 10021
(212) 988–7700

American Film Institute
John F. Kennedy Center for the Performing Arts
Washington, DC 20566
(202) 828–4044

American Film Institute
2021 N. Western Avenue
Los Angeles, CA 90027
(213) 856–7600

American Film Marketing Association
9000 Sunset Boulevard, Suite 515
Los Angeles, CA 90069
(213) 275–3400

American Guild of Musical Artists, Inc. (AAA–AFL)
1841 Broadway
New York, NY 10023
(212) 265–3687

American Guild of Variety Artists
184 Fifth Avenue
New York, NY 10010
(212) 675–1003

American Guild of Variety Artists
4741 Laurel Canyon Boulevard, Suite 208
North Hollywood, CA 91607
(818) 508–9984

American Indian Registry for the Performing Arts
3330 Barham Boulevard, Suite 708
Los Angeles, CA 90068
(213) 851–9874

American Radio Association
26 Journal Square, Suite 1501
Jersey City, NJ 07306
(201) 795–5536

American Society for Aesthetics
C. W. Post Center
Long Island University
Greenvale, NY 11548
(516) 299–2341

American Society for Theatre Research
Department of English
Queens College
Flushing, NY 11367
(212) 520–7462

American Society of Cinematographers, Inc.
1782 North Orange Drive
Hollywood, CA 90028
(213) 876–5080

American Society of Composers, Authors and Publishers (ASCAP)
One Lincoln Plaza
New York, NY 10023
(212) 595–3050

American Society of Lighting Directors, Inc.
4974 Hollywood Boulevard
Hollywood, CA 90028
(213) 663–1915

American Society of TV Cameramen
P.O. Box 296
Sparkill, NY 10976
(914) 359–5985

American Theatre Association
1010 Wisconsin Avenue NW, Sixth Floor
Washington, DC 20007
(202) 342–7350

American Theatre Critics Association
1860 Broadway, Suite 601
New York, NY 10023
(212) 289–5679

American Theatre Organ Society
4429 Pennsylvania Avenue
Fair Oaks, CA 95628

American Theatre Wing
681 Fifth Avenue
New York, NY 10022
(212) 759–5001

American Women in Radio and Television
1321 Connecticut Avenue NW
Washington, DC 20036
(202) 296–0009

American Writers Theatre Foundation
P.O. Box 810
Times Square Station
New York, NY 10036
(212) 581–5295

ANTA West
427 North Canyon Drive, Suite 216
Beverly Hills, CA 90210
(213) 273–2317

Archives of the Airwaves
Box 4
Needham, MA 02192

Armed Forces Broadcasters Association
P.O. Box 12013
Arlington, VA 22209
(202) 644–3511

Armed Forces Radio & TV Service
10888 La Tuna Canyon Road
Sun Valley, CA 91352
(818) 504–1201

Armstead-Johnson Foundation for Theatre Research
222 West 23 Street
New York, NY 10011

Art Directors Local 876 (IATSE)
7715 Sunset Boulevard
Hollywood, CA 90046
(213) 876–4330

ASIFA/Hollywood
5301 Laurel Canyon, Suite 250
North Hollywood, CA 91607
(818) 508–5224

Associated Actors and Artists of America (AFL-CIO)
165 West 46 Street
New York, NY 10019
(212) 869–0358

Associated Councils of the Arts
570 Seventh Avenue
New York, NY 10018
(212) 354–6655

Association for Broadcast Engineering Standards
2000 M Street NW, Suite 600
Washington, DC 20036
(202) 331–0606

Association of Film Craftsmen
Local 531, NABET, AFL-CIO, CLC
1800 North Argyle Street
Los Angeles, CA 90028
(213) 462–7484

Association of Independent Commercial Producers
2049 Century Park East
Los Angeles, CA 90067
(213) 553–9678

Association of Independent Video and Filmmakers
625 Broadway, 9th Floor
New York, NY 10012
(212) 473–3400

Association of Motion Picture Producers
8480 Beverly Boulevard
Los Angeles, CA 90048
(213) 653–2200

Association of Talent Agents
9255 Sunset Boulevard
Los Angeles, CA 90069
(213) 274–0628

Association of Theatrical Press Agents and Managers
268 West 47 Street
New York, NY 10036
(212) 582–3750

Astoria Motion Picture and Television Foundation
34–31 35th Street
Astoria, NY 11106
(212) 784–4520

Audio Engineering Society
60 East 42 Street
New York, NY 10165

Beyond Baroque Foundation
Old Venice City Hall
P.O. Box 806
621 Venice Boulevard
Venice, CA 90291
(213) 822–3006

Black American Cinema Society
3617 Montclair Street
Los Angeles, CA 90018
(213) 737–3292

Black Awareness in Television
13217 Livernois
Detroit, MI 48238
(313) 931–3427

Black Filmmakers Foundation
One Centre Street, Room 2711
New York, NY 10007
(212) 619–2480

Black Filmmakers Hall of Fame, Inc.
477 15 Street, Suite 200
Oakland, CA 94612
(415) 465–0804

Black Stuntmen's Association
8949 West 24 Street
Los Angeles, CA 90034
(213) 870–9020

Black Theatre Alliance
410 West 42 Street
New York, NY 10036
(212) 564–2266

British Film Institute
81 Dean Street
London W1V 6AA
England

British Film Institute
127 Charing Cross Road
London WC2 0EA
England
(01) 437–4355

British Theatre Association
9 Fitzroy Square
London W1P 6AE
England
(01) 387–2666

Broadcast Music Inc.
320 West 57 Street
New York, NY 10019
(212) 586–2000

Broadcast Pioneers
320 West 57 Street
New York, NY 10019
(212) 586–2000

Cable Television Information Center
1500 North Beauregard Street, Suite 205
Arlington, VA 22231
(703) 528–6836

Canadian Association of Broadcasters
165 Sparks Street, Eighth Floor
P.O. Box 627, Station B
Ottawa, Ontario K1P 5S2
Canada
(613) 233–4305

Canadian Association of Motion Picture Producers
P.O. Box 790, Station F
Toronto, Ontario M4Y 1T1
Canada
(416) 961–2288

Canadian Film Institute
75 Albert Street
Ottawa, Ontario K1P 5E7
Canada
(613) 232–6727

Canadian Society of Cinematographers
1589 The Queensway, Unit 14
Toronto, Ontario M8Z 5W9
Canada
(416) 251–2211

Cartoon/Fantasy Organization
401 South La Brea Avenue
Inglewood, CA 90301
(213) 412–2638

Casting Society of America
P.O. Box 8457
Universal City, CA 91608
(213) 203–3024

Catholic Actors Guild of America
1501 Broadway, Suite 2400
New York, NY 10036
(212) 398–1868

Catholic Conference, Department of Communication
1011 First Avenue, Suite 1300
New York, NY 10022
(212) 644–1898

Center for Arts Information
625 Broadway
New York, NY 10012
(212) 677–7548

Children's Theatre Association of America
1010 Wisconsin Avenue NE, Sixth Floor
Washington, DC 20007

Children's TV Workshop
One Lincoln Plaza
New York, NY 10023
(212) 595–3456

Community Antenna Television Association
3977 Chain Bridge Road
Fairfax, VA 22030
(703) 691–8875

Conference of State Cable Agencies
1100 Raymond Boulevard
Newark, NJ 07102
(201) 648–4009

Consortium of University Film Centers
c/o Audio Visual Services
330 Kent State University Library
Kent State University
Kent, OH 44242
(216) 672–3456

Corporation for Public Broadcasting
1111 16 Street NW
Washington, DC 20036
(202) 293–6160

Costume Designers Guild
Local 892 (IATSE)
14724 Ventura Boulevard
Sherman Oaks, CA 91403
(818) 905–1557

Costume Society of America
330 West 42 Street, Suite 1702
New York, NY 10036
(212) 563–5552

Council of Canadian Filmmakers
Box 1003, Station A
Toronto, Ontario M5W 1G5
Canada
(416) 961–3911

Council of Film Organizations
334 West 54 Street
Los Angeles, CA 90037
(213) 752–5811

Council of Stock Theatres
c/o Taplinger Associates
415 Madison Avenue
New York, NY 10036

Council on International Non-Theatrical Events (CINE)
1201 16 Street NW
Washington, DC 20036
(202) 785–1136

Country Music Hall of Fame and Museum
4 Music Square East
Nashville, TN 37203
(615) 256–1639

Cultural Information Service
15 West 24 Street, Tenth Floor
New York, NY 10010
(212) 691–5240

Directors Guild of America, Inc.
7950 Sunset Boulevard
Los Angeles, CA 90046
(213) 656–1220

Directors Guild of America, Inc.
110 West 57 Street
New York, NY 10019
(212) 581–0370

Directors Guild of America, Inc.
520 North Michigan Avenue
Chicago, IL 60611
(312) 644–5050

Directors Guild of Canada
3 Church Street, Suite 47
Toronto, Ontario M5E 1M2
Canada
(416) 364–0122

Drama Desk
c/o Alvin Klein
54 Charles Street
New York, NY 10014
(212) 242–1251

Drama League of New York, Inc.
1035 Fifth Avenue
New York, NY 10028
(212) 302–2100

Dramatists Guild, Inc
234 West 44 Street
New York, NY 10036
(212) 398–9366

Ecumedia
4270 West 6 Street, Suite 10
Los Angeles, CA 90020
(213) 380–0460

Educational Broadcasting Corporation
356 West 58 Street
New York, NY 10019
(212) 560–2000

Educational Film Library Association (EFLA)
45 John Street, Suite 301
New York, NY 10038
(212) 227–5599

Episcopal Actors Guild of America, Inc.
1 East 29 Street
New York, NY 10016
(212) 685–2927

Federal Communications Commission (FCC)
1919 M Street NW
Washington, DC 20054
(202) 655–4000

Federation of Motion Picture Councils
4792 Belfast Avenue
Oakland, CA 94619

Film Advisory Board
7080 Hollywood Boulevard, Suite 312
Hollywood, CA 90028
(213) 874–3644

Film Arts Foundation
346 Ninth Street, Second Floor
San Francisco, CA 94103
(415) 552–8760

Film Canada Center
144 South Beverly Drive, Suite 400
Beverly Hills, CA 90212
(213) 859–0268

Film Culture Non-Profit Corporation
491 Broadway
New York, NY 10012
(212) 226–0010

Film Library Information Council
Box 348, Radio City Station
New York, NY 10019
(212) 956–4211

Film Society of Lincoln Center
140 West 65 Street
New York, NY 10023
(212) 877–1800

Ford's Theatre Society
511 Tenth Street NW
Washington, DC 20004
(202) 638–2941

Foundation for Extension and Development of the
American Professional Theatre
165 West 46 Street
New York, NY 10036
(212) 869–9690

Foundation of Motion Picture Pioneers, Inc.
244 West 49 Street, Suite 305
New York, NY 10019
(212) 247–5588

Fred Astaire Performing Arts Association, Inc.
P.O. Box 560367
Miami, FL 33256
(305) 238–7911

French Film Office
745 Fifth Avenue
New York, NY 10151
(212) 832–8860

Friars Club
57 East 55 Street
New York, NY 10022
(212) 751–7272

Friars Club of California, Inc.
9900 Santa Monica Boulevard
Beverly Hills, CA 90212
(213) 879–3375

Friends of National Public Radio
P.O. Box 37603
Washington, DC 20013
(202) 466–4210

Gay Theatre Alliance
P.O. Box 294
New York, NY 10014
(212) 255–4713

176

George E. Nathan Trust
c/o Manufacturers Hanover Trust
600 Fifth Avenue
New York, NY 10020
(212) 350–4469

Golden Age Radio
Box 25215
Portland, OR 97225
(503) 297–6231

Golden Radio Buffs of Maryland, Inc.
7506 Iroquois Avenue
Baltimore, MD 21219
(301) 388–1976

Guild of Canadian Playwrights
The Writers' Center
24 Ryerson Avenue
Toronto, Ontario M5T 2P
Canada
(416) 868–6917

Harlem Performance Center
2394 Adam Clayton Powell Boulevard
New York, NY 10030

Hasty Pudding Theatricals
12 Holyoke Street
Cambridge, MA 02138
(617) 495–5205

Hebrew Actors Union
31 East 7 Street
New York, NY 10003
(212) 674–1923

Hollywood Comedy Club
2567 South Armacost
Los Angeles, CA 90064
(213) 479–0300

Hollywood Foreign Press Association
292 South La Cienega Boulevard, Suite 316
Beverly Hills, CA 90211
(213) 657–1731

Hollywood Stuntmen's Association
1043 Rafael Drive
Arcadia, CA 91006
(213) 478–8687

Hollywood Stuntmen's Union
6311 Romaine Street
Hollywood, CA 90038
(213) 462–0930

Illuminating Engineering Society of North America
345 East 47 Street
New York, NY 10017

Independent Feature Project/West
309 Santa Monica Boulevard, Suite 422
Santa Monica, CA 90401
(213) 451–8075

Independent Media Producers Association
1100 17 Street NW, Suite 1000
Washington, DC 20036
(202) 466–2175

Independent Motion Picture Producers Association
c/o Morris Landres
10501 Wilshire Boulevard, Suite 2111
Los Angeles, CA 90024
(213) 279–2187

Institute for Advanced Studies in the Theatre Arts
310 West 56 Street
New York, NY 10019
(212) 581–3133

Institute of Outdoor Drama
University of North Carolina
Chapel Hill, NC 27514
(919) 933–1328

Institute of the American Musical
121 North Detroit Street
Los Angeles, CA 90036
(213) 934–1221

Intercollegiate Broadcasting System
Box 592
Vails Gate, NY 12584
(914) 565–6710

Interlochen Center for the Arts
Interlochen, MI 49643
(616) 276–9221

International Alliance of Theatrical Stage Employes and Moving Picture
Machine Operators of the United States and Canada
1515 Broadway, Suite 601
New York, NY 10036
(212) 730–1770

International Association for Semiotic Studies
c/o Semiotics
3 Westchester Plaza
Elmsford, NY 10532

International Brotherhood of Electrical Workers (AFL)
1125 15 Street NW
Washington, DC 20005
(202) 833–7000

International Documentary Association (IDA)
8480 Beverly Boulevard, Suite 140
Los Angeles, CA 90048
(213) 655–7089

International Federation of Super 8 Cinema
9155 Rue St. Hubert
Montreal, Quebec H2M 1Y8
Canada
(514) 389–5921

International Film Seminars
23 West 43 Street, Suite 1118
New York, NY 10036
(212) 764–0032

International Foundation for Theatrical Research
P.O. Box 4526
Albuquerque, NM 87196
(505) 843–7749

International Photographers of the Motion Picture Industries
Local 659 (IATSE)
7715 Sunset Boulevard
Hollywood, CA 90046
(213) 876–0160

International Radio and Television Society, Inc.
420 Lexington Avenue, Suite 531
New York, NY 10170
(212) 867–6650

International Society for Optical Engineering
P.O. Box 10
Bellingham, WA 98227

International Society of Performing Arts Administrators
Performing Arts Center
P.O. Box 7818
University of Texas
Austin, TX 78712
(512) 471–2787

International Sound Technicians of the Motion Picture, Broadcast and
Amusement Industries
Local 695 (IATSE-AFL)
15840 Ventura Boulevard
Encino, CA 91436
(213) 872–0452

International Stunt Association
3518 Cahuenga Boulevard West, Suite 300
Hollywood, CA 90068
(213) 874–3174

International Teleproduction Society, Inc.
990 Avenue of the Americas, Suite 21 E
New York, NY 10018
(212) 629–3266

International Theatre Institute of the United States
1860 Broadway, Suite 1510
New York, NY 10023
(212) 245–3950

International Thespian Society
3368 Central Parkway
Cincinnati, OH 45225
(513) 559–1964

Iris Films/Iris Feminist Collective
Box 5353
Berkeley, CA 94705
(415) 549–3192

John F. Kennedy Center for the Performing Arts
Washington, DC 20566
(202) 872–0466

Joint Council on Educational Telecommunications
c/o Corporation for Public Broadcasting
1111 16 Street NW
Washington, DC 20036
(202) 293–6160

League of Historic American Theatres
1600 H Street NW
Washington, DC 20006
(202) 289–1494

League of New York Theatres and Producers
226 West 47 Street
New York, NY 10036
(212) 764–1122

League of Off-Broadway Theatres and Producers
c/o Circle in the Square
1633 Broadway
New York, NY 10019
(212) 581–3270

League of Resident Theatres
Center Stage
700 North Calvert Road
Baltimore, MD 21201
(301) 685–3200

Lincoln Center for the Performing Arts
140 West 65 Street
New York, NY 10023
(212) 877–1800

Los Angeles Drama Critics Circle
P.O. Box 38771
Los Angeles, CA 90038
(213) 464–5079

Los Angeles Film Critics Association
Times Mirror Square
Los Angeles, CA 90053
(213) 972–7000

Los Angeles Theatre Alliance
P.O. Box 481069
Los Angeles, CA 90049
(213) 386–2750

Make-Up Artists and Hair Stylists
Local 706 (IATSE)
11519 Chandler Boulevard
North Hollywood, CA 91601
(818) 984–1700

Make-Up Artists and Hair Stylists
Local 798 (IATSE)
1790 Broadway
New York, NY 10019
(212) 354–6016

The Masquers
940 South Figueroa Street
Los Angeles, CA 90028
(213) 874–0840

Media Commentary Council
1515 Broadway, Fourth Floor
New York, NY 10036
(212) 398–1300

Media Forum
P.O. Box 8156
North Hollywood, CA 91608
(213) 766–2490

Motion Picture and Television Fund
23388 Mulholland Drive
Woodland Hills, CA 91364
(818) 715–1155

Motion Picture Association of America, Inc.
1600 Eye Street NW
Washington, DC 20006
(202) 293–1966

Motion Picture Association of America, Inc.
1133 Avenue of the Americas
New York, NY 10036
(212) 840–6161

Motion Picture Association of America, Inc.
14144 Ventura Boulevard
Sherman Oaks, CA 91423
(818) 995–3600

Motion Picture Costumers
Local 705 (IATSE)
1527 North La Brea Avenue
Hollywood, CA 90028
(213) 851–0220

Motion Picture Editors Guild
Local 776 (IATSE)
7715 Sunset Boulevard
Hollywood, CA 90046
(213) 876–4770

Motion Picture Export Association of America
1133 Avenue of the Americas
New York, NY 10036
(212) 840–6161

Motion Picture Industry Pension Plan
P.O. Box 1766
Studio City, CA 91604
(818) 769–0081

Motion Picture Mothers, Inc.
c/o Motion Picture and Television Fund
23388 Mulholland Drive
Woodland Hills, CA 91364

Motion Picture Screen Cartoonists
Local 839 (IATSE)
4729 Lankershim Boulevard
North Hollywood, CA 91602
(818) 766–7151

Motion Picture Studio Art Craftsmen—Illustrators & Matte Artists
Local 790 (IATSE)
7715 Sunset Boulevard, Suite 210
Los Angeles, CA 90046
(213) 876–2010

Musicians Union
Local 47 (AFM, AFL-CIO)
817 Vine Street
Hollywood, CA 90038
(213) 462–2161

NABET/Association of Film Craftsmen
945 Front Street, Suite 201
San Francisco, CA 94111
(415) 956–5758

National Academy of Television Arts and Sciences
110 West 57 Street
New York, NY 10019
(212) 586–8424

National Arts Club
15 Gramercy Park
New York, NY 10003
(212) 475–3424

National Assembly of Local Arts Agencies
1785 Massachusetts Avenue NW
Washington, DC 20036
(202) 483–8670

National Association for Better Broadcasting
7918 Naylor Avenue
Los Angeles, CA 90045
(213) 641–4902

National Association of Black Owned Broadcasters
1730 M Street NW, Suite 708
Washington, DC 20036
(202) 463–8970

National Association of Broadcast Employees and Technicians
7101 Wisconsin Avenue, Suite 800
Bethesda, MD 20814
(301) 657–8420

National Association of Broadcasters
1771 N Street, NW
Washington, DC 20036
(202) 429–5300

National Association of Dramatic and Speech Arts
Fort Valley State College
Box 4579
Fort Valley, GA 31030
(912) 825–6217

National Association of Independent Television Producers and Distributors
375 Park Avenue, 30th Floor
New York, NY 10022
(212) 751–0600

National Association of Television Program Executives, Inc.
342 Madison Avenue, Suite 933
New York, NY 10017
(212) 949–9890

National Association of Theatre Owners
1560 Broadway, Suite 714
New York, NY 10036
(212) 730–7420

National Association of the Legitimate Theatre
226 West 47 Street
New York, NY 10036

National Black Theatre
9 East 125 Street
New York, NY 10035
(212) 427–5615

National Board of Review of Motion Pictures, Inc.
P.O. Box 589
New York, NY 10021
(212) 628–1594

National Cable Television Association
1724 Massachusetts Avenue NW
Washington, DC 20036
(202) 775–3550

National Cable Television Institute
P.O. Box 27277
Denver, CO 80227
(303) 761–8554

National Coalition of Television Violence
P.O. Box 2157
Champaign, IL 61820
(217) 359–8235

National Collegiate Players
Beloit College
Beloit, WI 53511
(608) 362–7141

National Costumers Association
Jester Costume Company
2616 Philadelphia Pike
Claymont, DE 19703
(302) 792–1883

National Council for the Arts and Education, Inc.
743 Fifth Avenue
New York, NY 10022
(212) 759–5800

National Endowment for the Arts
1100 Pennsylvania Avenue NW
Washington, DC 20506
(202) 682–5400

National Endowment for the Humanities
1100 Pennsylvania Avenue NW
Washington, DC 20506
(202) 786–0438

National Federation of Community Broadcasters
1314 14 Street NW
Washington, DC 20005
(202) 797–8911

National Foundation for Advancement in the Arts
100 North Biscayne Boulevard, Suite 1801
Miami, FL 33132
(305) 371–9470

National Institute for Music Theatre
John F. Kennedy Center for the Performing Arts
Washington, DC 20566
(202) 965–2800

National Institute of Arts and Letters
633 West 155 Street
New York, NY 10032
(212) 368–5900

National Playwrights Conference
1860 Broadway, Suite 601
New York, NY 10023
(212) 246–1485

National Video Clearinghouse, Inc.
100 Lafayette Drive
Syosset, NY 11791
(516) 364–3686

Negro Actors Guild
1674 Broadway
New York, NY 10003
(212) 972–7265

New England Theatre Conference
50 Exchange Street
Waltham, MA 02154
(617) 893–3120

New York Council of Motion Picture and Television Unions
326 West 48 Street
New York, NY 10036
(212) 757–8175

New York Drama Critics Circle
29 West 46 Street
New York, NY 10036
(212) 246–4314

North American Radio Archives
333 North Berendo Street
Fremont, CA 90004

North American Radio Archives
Box 15300
Flagstaff, AZ 86011

Nosostros
1314 North Wilton Place
Los Angeles, CA 90028
(213) 465–4167

Outer Critics Circle
c/o Charles K. Freeman
18 Overlook Road
Ossining, NY 10562
(212) 521–7777

Performing Arts Council
3701 West 54 Street
New York, NY 10043
(212) 972–7265

Permanent Charities Committee
463 North La Cienega Boulevard
Los Angeles, CA 90048
(213) 652–4680

Popular Culture Association
Popular Culture Center
Bowling Green University
Bowling Green, OH 43403
(419) 372–2981

Producers Guild of America, Inc.
292 South La Cienega Boulevard, Suite 205
Beverly Hills, CA 90211
(213) 659–6898

Public Broadcasting Service
475 L'Enfant Plaza West SW
Washington DC 20024
(202) 488–5000

Publicists Guild
Local 818 (IATSE)
14724 Ventura Boulevard, Penthouse 5
Sherman Oaks, CA 91403
(818) 905–1541

Radio Advertising Bureau
5900 Wilshire Boulevard, Suite 2200
Los Angeles, CA 90036
(213) 936–5515

Radio Advertising Bureau
485 Lexington Avenue
New York, NY 10017
(212) 599–6666

Radio Free Europe/Radio Liberty
1201 Connecticut Avenue NW
Washington, DC 20036
(202) 457–6900

Religious Arts Guild
25 Beacon Street
Boston, MA 02108
(617) 742–2100

Screen Actors Guild
7065 Hollywood Boulevard
Hollywood, CA 90028
(213) 465–4600

Screen Composers of America
2451 Nichols Canyon
Los Angeles, CA 90046
(213) 876–6040

Screen Extras Guild, Inc.
3629 Cahuenga Boulevard
Los Angeles, CA 90068
(213) 851–4301

Shubert Foundation
234 West 44 Street
New York, NY 10036
(212) 944–3777

Smithsonian Institution
Division of the Performing Arts
2100 L'Enfant Plaza
Washington, DC 20560
(202) 287–3420

Society for Cinema Studies
c/o Janice Welsch
Department of English
Western Illinois University
Macomb, IL 61445

Society for Imaging Science and Technology
7003 Kilworth Lane
Springfield, VA 22151

Society for the Preservation of Film Music
10850 Wilshire Boulevard, Suite 770
Los Angeles, CA 90024

Society of Broadcast Engineers
7002 Graham Road, Suite 118
Indianapolis, IN 46220
(317) 842–0836

Society of Cable Television Engineers
P.O. Box 2389
Westchester, PA 19380
(215) 692–7870

Society of Motion Picture and Television Art Directors
14724 Ventura Boulevard, No. 4
Sherman Oaks, CA 91403
(818) 905–0599

Society of Motion Picture and Television Engineers
595 West Hartsdale Avenue
White Plains, NY 10607–1824
(914) 761–1100

Society of Professional Stuntwomen
5501 Van Nord Avenue
Van Nuys, CA 91401
(818) 785–8988

Society of Stage Directors and Choreographers
1501 Broadway
New York, NY 10036
(212) 391–1070

Society of Television Pioneers
P.O. Box 1475
Lubbock, TX 79408
(806) 792–0404

Society of Wireless Pioneers, Inc.
Box 530
Santa Rosa, CA 95402
(707) 542–0898

Sons of the Desert
5151 White Oaks Avenue
Apartment 127
Encino, CA 91316

Sons of the Desert
P.O. Box 8341, East
Universal City, CA 91608
(818) 985–2713

Southeastern Theatre Conference, Inc.
1209 West Market Street
Greensboro, NC 27412
(919) 272–3645

Southwest Theatre Conference
Department of Speech and Drama
Southwest Texas State University
San Marcos, TX 78666

Speech Communication Association
5705 East Blacklick Road, No. E
Annendale, VA 22003
(703) 750–0533

Stuntmen's Association of Motion Pictures, Inc.
4810 Whitsett Avenue
North Hollywood, CA 91607
(818) 766–4334

Stuntwomen's Association of Motion Pictures, Inc.
202 Vance Street
Pacific Palisades, CA 90272
(213) 462–1605

Sundance Institute
19 Exchange Place
Salt Lake City, UT 84111
(801) 521–9330

Television Bureau of Advertising
6380 Wilshire Boulevard, Suite 1711
Los Angeles, CA 90048
(213) 653–8890

Television Critics Association
c/o Barbara Holsapple
Pittsburgh Press
34 Boulevard of the Allies
Pittsburgh, PA 15230
(412) 263–1100

Television Information Office
745 Fifth Avenue
New York, NY 10022
(212) 759–6800

Theatre Authority, Inc.
485 Fifth Avenue
New York, NY 10017
(212) 628–4215

Theatre Committee for Eugene O'Neill
1860 Broadway
New York, NY 10023
(212) 382–2790

Theatre Communications Group
355 Lexington Avenue
New York, NY 10017
(212) 697–5230

Theatre Development Fund
1501 Broadway
New York, NY 10036
(212) 221–0885

Theatre Guild—American Theatre Society
226 West 47 Street
New York, NY 10036
(212) 730–8080

Theatre Historical Society
c/o Dr. Robert K. Headley, Jr.
6510 41st Avenue North
Hyattsville, MD 20782
(219) 283–3615

Theatre Library Association
111 Amsterdam Avenue
New York, NY 10023
(212) 870–1670

Thomas A. Edison Papers
Rutgers, the State University of New Jersey
New Brunswick, NJ 08903
(201) 932–8511

The Troupers, Inc.
101 West 57 Street
New York, NY 10019
(212) 246–1500

United Nations Theatre Group
United Nations
New York, NY 10017
(212) 754–8321

United Scenic Artists
575 Eighth Avenue
New York, NY 10018
(212) 575–5120

University and College Theatre Association
1010 Wisconsin Avenue NW
Washington, DC 20007
(202) 342–7530

University Film and Video Association
Department of Cinema and Photography
Southern Illinois University
Carbondale, IL 62901
(618) 453–2365

University Film and Video Foundation
Department of Photography and Cinema
Ohio State University
Columbus, OH 43210
(614) 422–4920

Urban Arts Corps
26 West 20 Street
New York, NY 10011
(212) 924–7820

Urban Arts Theatre
227 West 17 Street
New York, NY 10011
(212) 924–7820

Variety Clubs International
Tower 58
Suite 23-C
58 West 58 Street
New York, NY 10019
(212) 751–8600

Video Alliance for the Performing Arts
c/o Homer Poupart
82 West 12 Street
New York, NY 10011
(212) 929–9107

Will Rogers Memorial Fund
785 Mamaroneck Avenue
White Plains, NY 10605
(914) 761–5501

Wolf Trap Foundation for the Performing Arts
1624 Trap Road
Vienna, VA 22180
(703) 938–3810

Women in Cable
2033 M Street NW
Washington, DC 20036
(202) 296–7245

Women in Film
8489 West 3 Street, Suite 25
Los Angeles, CA 90048
(213) 651–3680

Women in Show Business
P.O. Box 2535
North Hollywood, CA 91602
(818) 762–4669

Women in Theatre (WIT)
P.O. Box 3718
Los Angeles, CA 90078
(213) 461–6303

Women of the Motion Picture Industry (WOMPI)
940 7 Street
Santa Monica, CA 90403
(213) 471–4116

Women's International Theatre Alliance
6025 Cromwell Drive
Washington, DC 20016

Writers Guild of America, East
555 West 57 Street
New York, NY 10019
(212) 245–6180

Writers Guild of America, West
8955 Beverly Boulevard
Los Angeles, CA 90048
(213) 550–1000

Young Filmmakers Foundation
4 Rivington Street
New York, NY 10002
(212) 673–9361

Major U.S. Motion Picture and Television Studios and Production Companies _____

The following is a list of major American motion picture and television studios and production companies with their current main addresses and telephone numbers.

Aaron Spelling Productions, Inc.
1041 N. Formosa Avenue
West Hollywood, CA 90046
(213) 850–2500

Amblin Entertainment
100 Universal City Plaza
Bungalow 477
Universal City, CA 91608
(818) 777–4600

The Burbank Studios
4000 Warner Boulevard
Burbank, CA 91522
(818) 954–6000

The Cannon Group
640 San Vicente Boulevard
Los Angeles, CA 90038
(213) 658–2100

Columbia Pictures Corporation
Columbia Plaza
Burbank, CA 91505
(818) 954–6000

Concorde/New Horizons
11600 San Vicente Boulevard
Los Angeles, CA 90049
(213) 826–0978

Crown International Pictures
8701 Wilshire Boulevard
Beverly Hills, CA 90211
(213) 657–6700

DEG (De Laurentiis Entertainment Group)
8670 Wilshire Boulevard
Beverly Hills, CA 90211
(213) 854–7000

Embassy Communications
1901 Avenue of the Stars
Los Angeles, CA 90067
(213) 553–3600

Empire International
1551 North La Brea Avenue
Los Angeles, CA 90028
(213) 850–6663

Filmation Associates
6464 Canoga Avenue
Woodland Hills, CA 91367
(818) 712–4900

Fries Entertainment, Inc.
6922 Hollywood Boulevard, 12th Floor
Hollywood, CA 90028
(213) 466–2266

Hanna-Barbera Productions
3400 Cahuenga Boulevard
Los Angeles, CA 90068
(213) 851–5000

Hollywood Center Studios
1040 N. Las Palmas Avenue
Hollywood, CA 90028
(213) 469–5000

Island Pictures
9000 Sunset Boulevard, Suite 700
Los Angeles, CA 90069
(213) 276–4500

Kings Road Entertainment
1901 Avenue of the Stars, Suite 605
Los Angeles, CA 90067
(213) 552–0057

Laird International Studios
9336 W. Washington Boulevard
Culver City, CA 90232
(213) 836–5537

The Landsburg Company
11811 W. Olympic Boulevard
Los Angeles, CA 90064
(213) 478–7878

Lorimar-Telepictures Corporation
3970 Overland Avenue
Culver City, CA 90230
(213) 558–6497

Lucasfilm, Ltd.
P.O. Box 2009
San Rafael, CA 94912
(415) 662–1800

MCA TV
445 Park Avenue
New York, NY 10022
(212) 759–7500

Metro-Goldwyn-Mayer/UA Entertainment
11111 Santa Monica Boulevard, Suite 524
Los Angeles, CA 90025
(213) 444–1520

MTM Enterprises
4024 Radford Avenue
Studio City, CA 91604
(818) 760–5942

New World Pictures
1440 S. Sepulveda Boulevard
Los Angeles, CA 90025
(213) 444–8100

Orion Pictures Corporation
1875 Century Park East
Los Angeles, CA 90067
(213) 557–8701

Paramount Pictures Corporation
5555 Melrose Avenue
Los Angeles, CA 90038
(213) 468–5000

Raleigh Studios
650 N. Bronson Avenue
Los Angeles, CA 90038
(213) 466–3111

Republic Pictures Corporation
12636 Beatrice
Marina Del Rey, CA 90066
(213) 306–4040

RKO Pictures
1900 Avenue of the Stars, Suite 1562
Los Angeles, CA 90067
(213) 277–3133

The Samuel Goldwyn Company
10203 Santa Monica Boulevard
Los Angeles, CA 90067
(213) 552–2255

Stephen J. Cannell Productions
7083 Hollywood Boulevard
Hollywood, CA 90028
(213) 465–5800

Taft Entertainment Company
10960 Wilshire Boulevard
Los Angeles, CA 90024
(213) 208–2000

Trans-American Video
1541 Vine Street
Hollywood, CA 90028
(213) 466–2141

Tri-Star Pictures, Inc.
1875 Century Park East
Los Angeles, CA 90067
(213) 201–2300

Twentieth Century-Fox Film Corporation
P.O. Box 900
Beverly Hills, CA 90213
(213) 277–2211

United Artists Pictures
450 North Roxbury Drive
Beverly Hills, CA 90210
(213) 281–4000

Universal Pictures Corporation
100 Universal City Plaza
Universal City, CA 91608
(818) 777–4321

Viacom International, Inc.
10900 Wilshire Boulevard
Los Angeles, CA 90024
(213) 208–2700

The Walt Disney Company
500 S. Buena Vista Street
Burbank, CA 91503
(818) 840–1000

Warner Bros.
3901 W. Olive
Burbank, CA 91522
(818) 954–6000

Warner Bros. Hollywood Studios
1041 N. Formosa Avenue
West Hollywood, CA 90046
(213) 850–2500

Witt/Thomas Productions
846 Cahuenga Boulevard
Los Angeles, CA 90038
(213) 469–0575

U.S. Film Commissions _____

During the past several years the number of state and local film commissions within the United States and Canada has increased dramatically. This list includes the state and provincial film commissions, major metropolitan agencies, and selected international commissions. For a complete list of all domestic and international film commissions, contact:

The Association of Film Commissioners
One Paseo De San Antonio
San Jose, CA 95113
(408) 295–9600

LIST OF FILM COMMISSIONS OFFICES

Alabama Film Commission
340 N. Hull Street
Montgomery, AL 36130
(800) 633–5898

Alaska Motion Picture Development Office
3601 C Street, Suite 722
Anchorage, AK 99503
(907) 563–2167

Arizona Motion Picture Development Office
1700 W. Washington Avenue, Suite 330
Phoenix, AZ 85004
(602) 255–5011

Arkansas Motion Picture Development Office
One State Capitol Mall
Little Rock, AR 72201
(501) 371–7676

California Film Office
6922 Hollywood Boulevard, Suite 600
Hollywood, CA 90028
(213) 736–2465

Chicago Office of Film & Entertainment Industries
121 N. La Salle Street, Suite 810
Chicago, IL 60602
(312) 744–6415

Colorado Motion Picture & TV Commission
1313 Sherman Square, Suite 523
Denver, CO 80203
(303) 866–2778

Connecticut Film Commission
210 Washington Street
Hartford, CT 06106
(203) 566–7947

Delaware Development Office
99 Kings Highway
P.O. Box 1401
Dover, DE 19903
(800) 441–8846

DC Film Commission
District Building, Room 208
Washington, DC 20004–3001
(202) 727–6600

Florida Motion Picture & TV Bureau
107 W. Gaines Street
Tallahassee, FL 32301
(908) 487–1100

Georgia Film & Videotape Office
Department of Industry & Trade
230 Peachtree Street, NW
P.O. Box 1776
Atlanta, GA 30303
(404) 656–3591

Hawaii Film Industry Board
Department of Planning & Economic Development
P.O. Box 2359
Honolulu, HI 96804
(808) 548–4535

Idaho Film Bureau
Capitol Building, Room 108
Boise, ID 83720
(208) 334–4357

Illinois Film Office
100 W. Randolph Street, Suite 3–400
Chicago, IL 60601
(312) 917–3600

Indiana Film Commission
Department of Commerce
One North Capitol, Suite 700
Indianapolis, IN 46204
(317) 232–8829

Iowa Film Development Office
600 E. Court Avenue, Suite A
Des Moines, IA 50309
(515) 281–8319

Kansas Film Commission
Department of Economic Development
400 W. 8th, 5th Floor
Topeka, KS 66603
(913) 296–2009

Kentucky Film Office
Commonwealth of Kentucky
Berry Hill
Frankfort, KY 40601
(502) 564-FILM

City of Los Angeles
Film Coordination Office
6922 Hollywood Boulevard, Suite 600
Los Angeles, CA 90028
(213) 736–2465

Louisiana Film Industry Commission
Office of Commerce & Industry
P.O. Box 94185
Baton Rouge, LA 70804–9165
(504) 342–9165

Maine Film Commission
P.O. Box 8424
Portland, ME 04104
(207) 797–6991

Maryland Film Commission
45 Calvert Street
Annapolis, MD 21401
(301) 269–3577

Massachusetts Film Bureau
Department of Commerce & Development
100 Cambridge Street, 13th Floor
Boston, MA 02202
(617) 727–3330

Office of Film & TV Services
Michigan Department of Commerce
1200 6th Street, 19th Floor
Detroit, MI 48226
(313) 256–2000

Minnesota Motion Picture & Television Board, Inc.
100 N. 6th Street, Suite 478-A
Minneapolis, MN 55403
(612) 332–6493

Mississippi Film Office
1200 Walter Sillers Building
P.O. Box 849
Jackson, MS 39205
(601) 359–3037

Missouri Film Commission
P.O. Box 118
Jefferson City, MO 65102
(314) 751–9050

Montana Film Commission
Montana Promotions
Department of Commerce
1424 9th Avenue
Helena, MT 58701
(800) 548–3390

Nebraska Telecommunications & Information Center
1800 N. 33rd Street
P.O. Box 83111
Lincoln, NE 68501–3111
(402) 471–2593

Motion Picture Division
State of Nevada Commission on Economic Development
McCarran International Airport
Las Vegas, NV 89158
(702) 386–5287

New Hampshire Film & TV Bureau
Box 856
Concord, NH 03301
(603) 271–2598

New Jersey Motion Picture & TV Commission
Gateway One, Suite 510
Newark, NJ 07102
(201) 648–6279

New Mexico Film Commission
1050 Old Pecos Trail
Santa Fe, NM 87501
(800) 545–9871

Governor's Office for Motion Picture & Television Development
230 Park Avenue, Suite 1155
New York, NY 10169
(212) 309–0540

City Mayor's Office of Film, Theatre & Broadcasting
254 W. 5th Street
New York, NY 10019
(212) 489–6710

North Carolina Film Commission
430 Salisbury Street
Raleigh, NC 27611
(919) 733–9900

Public Information Division
North Dakota Economic Development Commission
Liberty Memorial Building
State Capitol Grounds
Bismark, ND 58505
(701) 224–2810

Ohio Film Bureau
P.O. Box 1001
Columbus, OH 43266–0101
(800) 848–1300

Oklahoma Film Office
6601 Broadway Extension
#5 Executive Park
Oklahoma City, OK 73116
(405) 521–3525

Film & Video Division
Oregon Economic Development Department
595 Cottage Street NE
Salem, OR 97310
(800) 547–7842

Pennsylvania Film Bureau
461 Forum Building
Harrisburg, PA 17120
(717) 787 5333

Institute of Film & Television
P.O. Box 2350
San Juan, Puerto Rico 00936
(809) 758–4747

Rhode Island Film Commission
150 Benefit Street
Providence, RI 02903
(401) 277–3456

San Francisco Film Commission
Motion Picture Coordinator
Mayor's Office, Room 200
San Francisco, CA 94102
(415) 558–4551

South Carolina Film Office
P.O. Box 927
1301 Gervais Street, 11th Floor
Columbia, SC 29202
(803) 758–3091

South Dakota Film Commission
711 Wells Street
Pierre, SD 57501
(800) 843–8000

Tennessee Film, Tape & Music Commission
320 Sixth Avenue North, 7th Floor
Nashville, TN 37219
(800) 251–8594

Texas Film Commission
P.O. Box 12728
Austin, TX 78711
(512) 469–9111

Utah Film Development
6150 State Office Building
Salt Lake City, UT 84114
(800) 453–8824

Vermont Film Bureau
Montpelier, VT 05602
(802) 828–3236

Virgin Islands Film Promotion Office
P.O. Box 6400
St. Thomas, VI 00801
(809) 774–8784

Virginia Film Office
Department of Economic Development
Washington Building
Richmond, VA 23219
(804) 786–3791

Washington State Film & Video Office
312 First Avenue N
Seattle, WA 98109
(206) 464–7148

West Virginia Department of Commerce
State Capitol Complex Building 6
Charleston, WV 25305
(800) 624–9110

Wisconsin Department of Development
Division of Tourism
123 W. Washington Avenue
Box 7970
Madison, WI 53707
(608) 267–7176

Wyoming Film Commission
Interstate 25 and College Drive
Cheyenne, WY 82002–0660
(307) 777–7851

International Film Commissions _____

AUSTRALIA

Australian Film Commission
8 West Street
North Sydney
New South Wales 2060
Australia
(02) 922–6855

BAHAMAS

Bahamas Film Commission
P.O. Box N3701
Nassau
Bahamas
(809) 322–1656

CANADA

Alberta Film Industry Economic Development
9940 106th Street
10th Floor, Sterling Place
Edmonton, Alberta
Canada T5K 2P6
(403) 427–2005

British Columbia Film Promotion Office
800 Hornby Street
Suite 222
Vancouver, British Columbia
Canada V6Z 2C5
(604) 660–2732

Manitoba Culture, Heritage and Recreation
177 Lombard Avenue
4th Floor
Winnipeg, Manitoba
Canada R3B 0W5
(204) 945–8828

City of Montreal Film Commission
155 Notre Dame Street, East #224
Montreal, Quebec
Canada H2Y 1B5
(514) 872–2883

National Film Board of Canada
Operations Headquarters
125 Houde
Ville St-Laurent, Quebec
Canada H4N 2J3
(514) 333–4500

Nova Scotia Film Resources Center
1531 Grafton Street
Halifax, Nova Scotia
Canada B3J 2B9
(902) 422–3402

Ontario Film Development Corporation
81 Wellesley Street East
Toronto, Ontario
Canada M4Y 1H6
(416) 965–6392

Saskatchewan Department of Development and Trade
Bank of Montreal Building
2103 11th Avenue
Regina, Saskatchewan
Canada S4P 3V7
(306) 787–2172

IRELAND

Irish Film Board
65 Pembroke Lane
Dublin 2
Eire
687033

JAMAICA

Jamaican National Investment Promotion, Ltd.
15 Oxford Road
Kingston 5
Jamaica
(809) 926–4613

NEW ZEALAND

New Zealand Film Commission
P.O. Box 11546
56 Courtenay Place
Wellington
New Zealand
(4) 859754

Television Networks _____

The following is a list of the three national television networks and the major independent and cable television networks within the United States, with the addresses of their corporation headquarters and their telephone numbers.

ABC, Inc. (American Broadcasting Corporation)
1300 Avenue of the Americas
New York, NY 10019
(212) 887–7777

ABC, Inc.
4151 Prospect Avenue
Los Angeles, CA 90027
(213) 557–7777

The Arts and Entertainment Network
555 Fifth Avenue
New York, NY 10017
(212) 661–4500

Cable News Network (CNN)
1050 Techwood Drive NW
Atlanta, GA 30318
(404) 827–1500

CBS, Inc. (Columbia Broadcasting System)
51 W. 52nd Street
New York, NY 10019
(212) 975–4321

CBS, Inc.
7800 Beverly Boulevard
Los Angeles, CA 90036
(213) 852–2345

The Disney Channel
3800 West Alameda Boulevard
Burbank, CA 91505
(818) 569–7500

Fox Broadcasting Company
10201 W. Pico Boulevard
Los Angeles, CA 90035
(213) 277–2211

Golden West Broadcasting
5800 West Sunset Boulevard
Los Angeles, CA 90028
(213) 460–5500

HBO (Home Box Office, Inc.)
2049 Century Park East, Suite 4100
Los Angeles, CA 90067
(213) 201–9300

NBC, Inc. (National Broadcasting Corporation)
30 Rockefeller Plaza
New York, NY 10112
(212) 664–4444

NBC, Inc.
3000 W. Alameda Avenue
Burbank, CA 91523
(818) 840–4444

PBS (Public Broadcasting Service)
1320 Braddock Place
Alexandria, VA 22313
(703) 739–5333

Showtime/The Movie Channel, Inc.
10900 Wilshire Boulevard
Los Angeles, CA 90024
(213) 208–2340

Tribune Entertainment Company
435 N. Michigan Avenue, Room 1429
Chicago, IL 60611
(312) 222–4484

Turner Broadcasting System
1050 Techwood Drive NW
Atlanta, GA 30318
(404) 827–1500

Westinghouse Broadcasting Company (Group W)
90 Park Avenue
New York, NY 10016
(212) 983–6500

Index _____

About the Compilers

ANTHONY SLIDE, film scholar and historian, is the author of more than thirty volumes on the history of the performing arts, including *International Film, Radio, and Television Journals, The American Film Industry: A Historical Dictionary* (Greenwood Press, 1985, 1986), *A Collector's Guide to Movie Memorabilia*, and *The Vaudevillians*. His numerous articles have appeared in such journals as *Emmy, American Cinematographer*, and *Films in Review*.

PATRICIA KING HANSON is editor of the American Film Institute Catalog of Feature Films, 1911–1920 and 1931–1940. She was co-editor (with Stephen Hanson) of the four-volume *Magill's Bibliography of Literary Criticism*, the thirteen-volume *Magill's Survey of Cinema*, and *Magill's Cinema Annual*. She is also film reviewer for the pre-eminent British film trade journal, *Screen International*.

STEPHEN L. HANSON is Assistant Head of the Reference Department for the University Library at the University of Southern California. He was co-editor (with Patricia King Hanson) of *Magill's Bibliography of Literary Criticism, Magill's Survey of Cinema*, and *Magill's Cinema Annual*. He is also film reviewer for the British trade journal *Screen International*.